Learn Unity ML-Agents – Fundamentals of Unity Machine Learning

Incorporate new powerful ML algorithms such as Deep Reinforcement Learning for games

Micheal Lanham

BIRMINGHAM - MUMBAI

Learn Unity ML - Agents - Fundamentals of Unity Machine Learning

Commissioning Editor: Kunal Chaudhari
Acquisition Editor: Reshma Raman
Content Development Editor: Roshan Kumar
Technical Editor: Shweta Jadhav
Copy Editor: Safis Editing
Project Coordinator: Hardik Bhinde
Proofreader: Safis Editing
Indexer: Rekha Nair
Graphics: Jason Monteiro
Production Coordinator: Shraddha Falebhai

First published: June 2018

Production reference: 1290618

Published by Packt Publishing Ltd.
Livery Place
35 Livery Street
Birmingham
B3 2PB, UK.

ISBN 978-1-78913-813-9

www.packtpub.com

To my mentors, Dr. Peter Daly, Pat McLellan, and Uncle Herb (Ewing), for their support and guidance

– Micheal Lanham

`mapt.io`

Mapt is an online digital library that gives you full access to over 5,000 books and videos, as well as industry leading tools to help you plan your personal development and advance your career. For more information, please visit our website.

Why subscribe?

- Spend less time learning and more time coding with practical eBooks and Videos from over 4,000 industry professionals

- Improve your learning with Skill Plans built especially for you

- Get a free eBook or video every month

- Mapt is fully searchable

- Copy and paste, print, and bookmark content

PacktPub.com

Did you know that Packt offers eBook versions of every book published, with PDF and ePub files available? You can upgrade to the eBook version at `www.PacktPub.com` and, as a print book customer, you are entitled to a discount on the eBook copy. Get in touch with us at `service@packtpub.com` for more details.

At `www.PacktPub.com`, you can also read a collection of free technical articles, sign up for a range of free newsletters, and receive exclusive discounts and offers on Packt books and eBooks.

Contributors

About the author

Micheal Lanham is a proven software architect with 20 years' experience of developing a range of software, including games, mobile, graphic, web, desktop, engineering, GIS, and machine learning applications for various industries. In 2000, Micheal began working with machine learning and would later use various technologies for a broad range of apps, from geomechanics to inspecting pipelines in 3D. He was later introduced to Unity and has been an avid developer and author of multiple Unity apps and books since.

This book would not be possible without the efforts of the machine learning team at Unity, especially Dr. Danny Lange and Dr. Arthur Juliani.

Thanks to the editorial team at Packt for their assistance and support of my vision for this book. They, and the dedicated hardworking reviewers, make these books possible. I would also like to thank my home support team of Rhonda, my children, and my mother.

About the reviewers

Michael Oakes has worked in the IT industry for over 18 years and is a graduate from the University of Westminster and a Unity Certified Developer.

He is currently working as an augmented/virtual reality consultant and AI developer with a Canadian mobile company, and with his own company, Canunky Solutions, developing custom augmented/virtual reality and AI applications. Originally from Grimsby in the UK (home to his beloved Mariners football team), he now lives in Calgary, Canada, with his wife, Camie, and two cats (Peanut and Sammy).

Casey Cupp is a software developer with a focus on customer-based problem solving using full-stack technologies. He has worked on sustainable development in multitier data applications with an emphasis on utilizing GIS and machine learning technologies. He is the Lead Developer for Petroweb in the oil and gas data management industry, and a senior developer for Sales Temperature, a machine learning start-up in retail forecasting.

Packt is searching for authors like you

If you're interested in becoming an author for Packt, please visit `authors.packtpub.com` and apply today. We have worked with thousands of developers and tech professionals, just like you, to help them share their insight with the global tech community. You can make a general application, apply for a specific hot topic that we are recruiting an author for, or submit your own idea.

Table of Contents

Preface

Machine learning (ML) has been described as the next technological wave to hit humankind, akin to that of electricity. While this is a big claim, we can make certain analogies between the two technologies. For one, you really don't need to understand the inner workings of electricity to use it, and in some ways that applies to ML and many of the more advanced concepts. If you wire up a light the wrong way, it won't work, or you could hurt yourself, and the same analogy applies to machine learning. You still need enough knowledge to call yourself an MLtician or ML practitioner (if you will), and it is the goal of this book to give you that depth of knowledge. Now, the area of ML is broad, so our focus in this book will be to use deep reinforcement learning (DRL) in the form of Unity ML-Agents. DRL is currently a hot topic for developing robotic and simulation agents in many areas, and it is certainly a great addition to the Unity platform.

Who this book is for

This book is for anyone who wants a good practical introduction to some specific ML technologies that work and are very fun to play with. While this book covers some very advanced topics, anyone with a high-school level of math, patience, and understanding of C# will be able to work through all the exercises. We do feature example Python code and use Python for most of the training, but only a superficial knowledge of the language is required.

What this book covers

Chapter 1, *Introducing Machine Learning and ML-Agents*, covers the basics of machine learning and introduces the ML-Agents framework within Unity. This is basically just a setup chapter, but it's essential to anyone new to Unity and/or ML-Agents.

Chapter 2, *The Bandit and Reinforcement Learning*, introduces many of the basic problems and solutions used to teach reinforcement learning, from the multiarm and contextual bandit problems to a newly-derived connected bandit problem.

Chapter 3, *Deep Reinforcement Learning with Python*, explores the Python toolset available for your system and explains how to install and set up those tools. Then, we will cover the basics of neural networks and deep learning before coding up a simple reinforcement learning example.

Chapter 4, *Going Deeper with Deep Learning*, sets up ML-Agents to use the external Python trainers to create some fun but powerful agents that learn to explore and solve problems.

Chapter 5, *Playing the Game*, explains that ML-Agents is all about creating games and simulation in Unity. So, in this chapter, we will focus on various play strategies for training and interacting with agents in a real game or simulation.

Chapter 6, *Terrarium Revisited and a Multi-Agent Ecosystem*, revisits a coding game developed previously called Terrarium as a way to build self-learning agents who live in a little ecosystem. We learn how game rules can be applied to building a game or simulation with multiple agents that interact together.

To get the most out of this book

The following is a short list of the tools and attributes that may make you more successful as you explore this book:

- **Computer:** A desktop computer capable of running Unity, but all the samples are basic enough that even a low-end machine should be sufficient. Check the Unity documentation for the minimum requirements to run Unity.
- **Patience**: You may need to train agents for several hours, so expect to wait. Just remember that *your patience will be rewarded* (Alton Brown*)*. The better your machine, the less you wait, so there's also that.
- **GPU**: Don't fret if your computer does not have a support GPU to run TensorFlow; you can run the samples without it. It is nice to have, though.
- **High-school math**: If you need to brush up, basic statistics, algebra, and geometry should be sufficient. Developing your own apps will certainly benefit from a better understanding of the mathematics.
- **Programming**: A basic understanding of C# is required. You will find it helpful if you also know Unity and Python, but this is not required to run the exercises.

Download the example code files

You can download the example code files for this book from your account at www.packtpub.com. If you purchased this book elsewhere, you can visit www.packtpub.com/support and register to have the files emailed directly to you.

You can download the code files by following these steps:

1. Log in or register at www.packtpub.com.
2. Select the **SUPPORT** tab.
3. Click on **Code Downloads & Errata**.
4. Enter the name of the book in the **Search** box and follow the onscreen instructions.

Once the file is downloaded, please make sure that you unzip or extract the folder using the latest version of:

- WinRAR/7-Zip for Windows
- Zipeg/iZip/UnRarX for Mac
- 7-Zip/PeaZip for Linux

The code bundle for the book is also hosted on GitHub at https://github.com/ PacktPublishing/Learn-Unity-ML-Agents-Fundamentals-of-Unity-Machine-Learning. In case there's an update to the code, it will be updated on the existing GitHub repository.

We also have other code bundles from our rich catalog of books and videos available at https://github.com/PacktPublishing/. Check them out!

Download the color images

We also provide a PDF file that has color images of the screenshots/diagrams used in this book. You can download it here: https://www.packtpub.com/sites/default/files/ downloads/LearnUnityMLAgentsFundamentalsofUnityMachineLearning_ColorImages.pdf.

Conventions used

There are a number of text conventions used throughout this book.

`CodeInText`: Indicates code words in text, database table names, folder names, filenames, file extensions, pathnames, dummy URLs, user input, and Twitter handles. Here is an example: " This command will create a new 3.5 Python environment named `[-n]` `mlagents`. "

A block of code is set as follows:

```
void Defend()
    {
      currentAction = "Defend";
      nextAction = Time.timeSinceLevelLoad + (25 / MaxSpeed);
    }
```

Any command-line input or output is written as follows:

```
conda activate ml-agents
```

Bold: Indicates a new term, an important word, or words that you see on screen. For example, words in menus or dialog boxes appear in the text like this. Here is an example: "Select **System info** from the **Administration** panel."

 Warnings or important notes appear like this.

 Tips and tricks appear like this.

Get in touch

Feedback from our readers is always welcome.

General feedback: Email feedback@packtpub.com and mention the book title in the subject of your message. If you have questions about any aspect of this book, please email us at questions@packtpub.com.

Errata: Although we have taken every care to ensure the accuracy of our content, mistakes do happen. If you have found a mistake in this book, we would be grateful if you would report this to us. Please visit www.packtpub.com/submit-errata, selecting your book, clicking on the Errata Submission Form link, and entering the details.

Piracy: If you come across any illegal copies of our works in any form on the internet, we would be grateful if you would provide us with the location address or website name. Please contact us at copyright@packtpub.com with a link to the material.

If you are interested in becoming an author: If there is a topic that you have expertise in and you are interested in either writing or contributing to a book, please visit authors.packtpub.com.

Reviews

Please leave a review. Once you have read and used this book, why not leave a review on the site that you purchased it from? Potential readers can then see and use your unbiased opinion to make purchase decisions, we at Packt can understand what you think about our products, and our authors can see your feedback on their book. Thank you!

For more information about Packt, please visit packtpub.com.

Introducing Machine Learning and ML-Agents

1

All around us, our perception of learning and intellect is being challenged daily with the advent of new and emerging technologies. From self-driving cars, playing Go and Chess, to computers being able to beat humans at classic Atari games, the advent of a group of technologies we colloquially call Machine Learning have come to dominate a new era in technological growth – a new era of growth that has been compared with the same importance as the discovery of electricity and has already been categorized as the next human technological age.

This book is intended to introduce you to a very small slice of that new era in a fun and informative way using the Machine Learning Agents platform called ML-Agents from Unity. We will first explore some basics of Machine Learning and ML-Agents. Then, we will cover training and specifically Reinforcement Learning and Q Learning. After that, we will learn how to use Keras to build a Neural Network that we will evolve into a Deep Q-Network. From there, we will look at various ways to improve the Deep Q-Network with different training strategies. This will lead us to our first example, where we train an agent to play a more complex game. Then, finally, we will finish with a look at a multi-agent example that allows agents to compete with or against each other.

 Machine Learning is a big subject and could certainly take years to master. You certainly won't learn everything you need to know from this book. This book is intended only as an enjoyable introduction to a complex and frustrating topic. We will try and point out other areas for learning more about certain techniques or backgrounds.

In our first chapter, we will take a gradual introduction to ML and ML-Agents. Here is what we will cover in this chapter:

- Machine Learning
- ML-Agents
- Running an example
- Creating an environment
- Academy, Agent, and Brain

Let's get started, and in the next section, we will introduce what Machine Learning is and the particular aspect of ML we plan to focus on in this book.

 If you have not already done so, be sure to download and install the latest version of Unity (https://unity3d.com/). Make sure you have the latest released version of the software and avoid any beta versions. We will use the Personal version in this book, but any version of Unity should work fine.

Machine Learning

Games and simulations are no stranger to AI technologies and there are numerous assets available to the Unity developer in order to provide simulated machine intelligence. These technologies include content like Behavior Trees, Finite State Machine, navigation meshes, A*, and other heuristic ways game developers use to simulate intelligence. So, why Machine Learning and why now? After all, many of the base ML techniques, like neural nets, we will use later in this book have been used in games before.

The reason, is due in large part to the OpenAI initiative, an initiative that encourages research across academia and the industry to share ideas and research on AI and ML. This has resulted in an explosion of growth in new ideas, methods, and areas for research. This means for games and simulations that we no longer have to fake or simulate intelligence. Now, we can build agents that learn from their environment and even learn to beat their human builders.

Machine Learning is an implementation of Artificial Intelligence. It is a way for a computer to assimilate data or state and provide a learned solution or response. We often think of AI now as a broader term to reflect a "smart" system. A full game AI system, for instance, may incorporate ML tools combined with more classic AIs like Behavior Trees in order to simulate a richer, more unpredictable AI. We will use AI to describe a system and ML to describe the implementation.

Training models

Machine Learning is so aptly named because it uses various forms of training to analyze data or state and provide that trained response. These methods are worth mentioning and we will focus on one particular method of learning that is currently showing good success. Before we get to that though, for later chapters, let's breakdown the three types of training we frequently see in ML:

- **Unsupervised Training**: This method of training examines a dataset on its own and performs a classification. The classification may be based on certain metrics and can be discovered by the training itself. Most people used to think that all AI or ML worked this way, but of course, it does not:
    - **ESRI**, which is a major mapping provider of GIS software and data provides a demographic dataset called **Tapestry**. This dataset is derived from a combination of US census data and other resources. It is processed through an ML algorithm that classifies the data into 68 consumer segments using Unsupervised Training. The Tapestry data is not free but can be invaluable for anyone building ML for a consumer or retail application.
- **Supervised Training**: This is the typical training method most data science ML methods use to perform prediction or classification. It is a type of training that requires input and output data be labelled. As such, it requires a set of training data in order to build a model. Oftentimes, depending on the particular ML technique, it can require vast amounts of data:
    - **Google Inception** is an image classification ML model that is freely available. It has been trained by millions of images into various trained classifications. The Inception model is small enough to fit on a mobile device in order to provide real-time image classification.

- **Reinforcement Learning**: This is based on control theory and provides a method of learning without any initial state or model of the environment. This is a powerful concept because it eliminates the need to model the environment or undertake the tedious data labeling often required by Supervised Training. Instead, agents are modeled in the environment and receive rewards based on their actions. Of course, that also means that this advanced method of training is not without its pitfalls and frustrations. We will start learning the details of RL in Chapter 2, *The Bandit and Reinforcement Learning*:
  - **DeepMind** built the bot that was able to play classic Atari 2600 games better than a human.

- **Imitation Learning**: This is a technique where agents are trained by watching a demonstration of the desired actions and then imitating them. This is a powerful technique and has plenty of applications. We will explore this type of training in Chapter 4, *Going Deeper with Deep Learning*.
- **Curriculum Learning**: This is an advanced form of learning that works by breaking down a problem into levels of complexity, which allows the agent or ML to overcome each level of complexity before moving on to more advanced activities. For example, an agent waiter may first need to learn to balance a tray, then the tray with a plate of food, then walking with the tray and food, and finally delivering the food to a table. We will explore this form of training in Chapter 5, *Playing the Game*.
- **Deep Learning**: This uses various forms of internal training mechanisms to train a multi-layer neural network. We will spend more time on neural networks and Deep Learning in Chapter 3, *Deep Reinforcement Learning with Python*.

You may have already noticed the interchange of terms ML and agent use to denote the thing that is learning. It is helpful to think of things in these terms for now. Later in this chapter, we will start to distinguish the differences between an agent and their brain or ML. For now, though, let's get back to some basics and explore a simple ML example in the next section.

A Machine Learning example

In order to demonstrate some of these concepts in a practical manner, let's look at an example scenario where we use ML to solve a game problem. In our game, we have a cannon that shoots a projectile at a specific velocity in a physics-based world. The object of the game is to choose the **velocity** to hit the target at a specific distance. We have already fired the cannon ten times and recorded the results in a table and chart, as shown in the following screenshot:

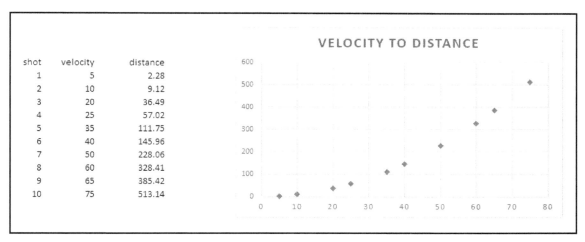

Record and chart of cannon shots

Since the data is labelled already, this problem is well-suited for Supervised Training. We will use a very simple method called linear regression in order to give us a model that can predict a velocity in order to hit a target at a certain distance. Microsoft Excel provides a quick way for us to model linear regression on the chart by adding a trendline, as follows:

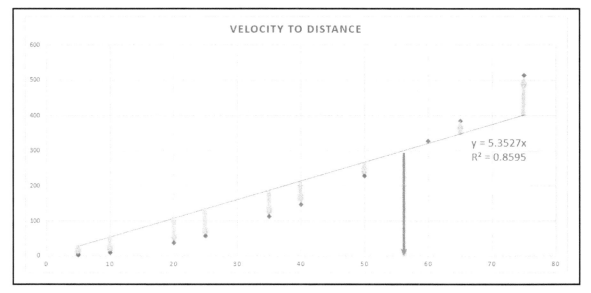

Linear Regression applied with a trendline

By using this simple feature in Excel, you can quickly analyze your data and see an equation that best fits that data. Now, this is a rudimentary example of data science, but hopefully you can appreciate how this can easily be used to predict complex environments just based on the data. While the linear regression model can provide us with an answer, it obviously is not very good and the R^2 reflects that. The problem we have with our model is that we are using a linear model to try and solve a nonlinear problem. This is reflected with the arrows to the points, where the distance shows the amount of errors from the trendline. Our goal with any ML method will be to minimize the errors in order to find the solution of best fit. In most cases, that is all ML is, finding an equation that best predicts/classifies a value or action.

Getting back to our earlier question, we can now solve the velocity using some simple algebraic substitution, as shown in the following equation:

$$d = 5.3527v$$

Where d = distance and v = velocity:

$$v = d/5.3527$$

$$v = 300/5.3527 = 56.05$$

Our final answer would be an answer of 56.05, but as we already mentioned, we may still miss, because our model is not entirely accurate. However, if you look at the graph, our errors appear to minimize around the distance of 300. So, in our specific example, our model fits well. Looking closer at the graph, though, you can see that at a distance of around 100, our error gets quite large and it is unlikely that we will hit our target.

 R^2 or R squared is an error value between 0 and 1, with 1 being the highest or best fit. R^2 attempts to summarize the quality of fit. In some cases, it works well and in others there are other measures of fit that work better. We will use different measures of quality of fitness, but the concepts are similar.

The example we just looked at is quite simple and doesn't take into account many other factors, such as elevation differences or movement speed, and so on. If we wanted to add those inputs, we would just add more columns to our table. Each new column would expand our data space and consequently increase the complexity of the model. As you can quickly see, our model could quickly expand and become impractical. This is essentially the shortcomings the gaming industry already experienced using ML techniques at the turn of the century when implementing game AI. It is also a shortcoming that any other industry faces when implementing supervision-based models. That is the need to constantly re-sample and relabel data and consequently retrain models, which is why Reinforcement Learning and other methods of learning have become so significant. They provide a method of learning whereby autonomous agents or ML with no previous knowledge of an environment can successfully explore.

ML uses in gaming

Unity has embraced the idea of incorporating ML into all aspects of its product and not just for use as a game AI. While most developers may try to use ML for gaming, it certainly helps game development in the following areas:

- **Map/Level Generation**: There are already plenty of examples where developers have used ML to auto-generate everything from dungeons to realistic terrain. Getting this right can provide a game with endless replayability, but it can be some of the most challenging ML to develop.
- **Texture/Shader Generation**: Another area that is getting the attention of ML is texture and shader generation. These technologies are getting a boost brought on by the attention of advanced generative adversarial networks, or GAN. There are plenty of great and fun examples of this tech in action; just do a search for DEEP FAKES in your favorite search engine.
- **Model Generation**: There are a few projects coming to fruition in this area that could greatly simplify 3D object construction through enhanced scanning and/or auto-generation. Imagine being able to textually describe a simple model and having ML build it for you, in real-time, in a game or other *AR*/VR/MR app, for example.
- **Audio Generation**: Being able to generate audio sound effects or music on the fly is already being worked on for other areas, not just games. Yet, just imagine being able to have a custom designed soundtrack for your game developed by ML.

- **Artificial Players**: This encompasses many uses from the gamer themselves using ML to play the game on their behalf to the developer using artificial players as enhanced test agents or as a way to engage players during low activity. If your game is simple enough, this could also be a way of auto testing levels, for instance. We will explore an example of using ML to play a game in Chapter 5, *Playing the Game*.
- **NPCs or Game AI**: Currently, there are better patterns out there to model basic behavioral intelligence in the form of Behavior Trees. While it's unlikely that BTs or other similar patterns will go away any time soon, imagine being able to model an NPC that may actually do an unpredictable, but rather cool behavior. This opens all sorts of possibilities that excite not only developers but players as well. We will look at ways of modeling behavioral patterns using ML in Chapter 6, *Terrarium Revisited – Building A Multi-Agent Ecosystem*.

Our interest in this book will be in the area of artificial players and the game AI, as it tends to be the most broad topic in scope. The reader is encouraged to search out the other areas mentioned in the preceding list on their own and as/when they relate to their own project.

It is highly recommended that you take a course, read a book, or watch a video on **Data Science**. The area of data science deals primarily with Supervised and Unsupervised Training on ML against known datasets. However, you will or should learn data scrubbing, data labeling, the mathematics of ML, and calculating errors to name just a few important concepts. Having a background in Data Science will help you model problems as well as help you uncover possible issues when things don't work as expected.

That overview of ML certainly won't rival any Data Science course, but it should get us started for the rest of the good stuff starting in the next section, where we start looking at ML in action with Unity ML-Agents.

ML-Agents

For the rest of this book, we will be using the ML-Agents platform with Unity to build ML models that we can learn to play and simulate in various environments. Before we do that, though, we need to pull down the ML-Agents package from GitHub using git. Jump on your computer and open up a command prompt or shell window and follow along:

 If you have never used git before, make sure to install it from https:// git-scm.com/. You will need to install git before continuing with the following exercises and thus the rest of this book.

1. Navigate to your work or root folder (on Windows, we will assume that this is C:\):

```
cd/
```

2. Execute the following command:

```
mkdir ML-Agents
```

3. This will create the folder ML-Agents. Now, execute the following:

```
cd ML-Agents
git clone https://github.com/Unity-Technologies/ml-agents.git
```

4. This uses git to pull down the required files for ML-Agents into a new folder called ml-agents. git will show the files as they are getting pulled into the folder. You can verify that the files have been pulled down successfully by changing to the new folder and executing:

```
cd ml-agents
dir
```

5. Right now, we are doing this to make sure that there are any files here. We will get to the specifics later.

Good—that should have been fairly painless. If you had issues pulling the code down, you can always visit the ML-Agents page on GitHub at https://github.com/Unity-Technologies/ml-agents and manually pull the code down. Of course, we will be using more of git to manage and pull files, so you should resolve any problems you may have encountered.

If you are not familiar with GitHub and git, then you really should be. git completely dominates source control across all areas of software development now and is widely used, even at Microsoft, who abandoned their own source control for it. Do yourself a favor, even if you develop your code just for yourself: use source control.

Now that we have ML-Agents installed, we will take a look at one of Unity's sample projects that ships with a toolkit in the next section.

Running a sample

Unity ships the ML-Agents package with a number of prepared samples that demonstrate various aspects of learning and training scenarios. Let's open up Unity and load up a sample project and get a feel for how the ML-Agents run by following this exercise:

1. Open the Unity editor and go to the starting **Project** dialog.

2. Click the **Open** button at the top of the dialog and navigate to and select the ML-Agents/ml-agents/unity-environment folder, as shown in the following screenshot:

Loading the unity-environment project into the editor

3. This will load the `unity-environment` project into the Unity editor. Depending on the Unity version you are using, you may get a warning that the version needs to be upgraded. As long as you are using a recent version of Unity, you can just click Continue. If you do experience problems, try upgrading or downgrading your version of Unity.

4. Locate the `Scene` file in the `Assets/ML-Agents/Examples/3DBall` folder of the **Project** window, as shown in the following screenshot:

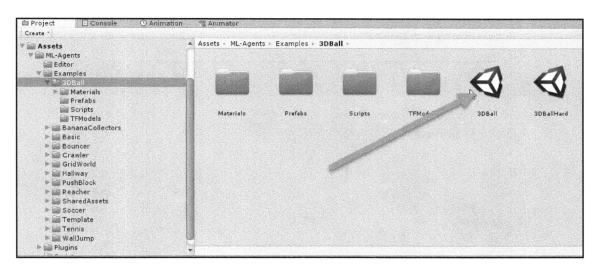

Locating the example scene file in the 3DBall folder

5. Double-click the `3DBall` scene file to open the scene in the editor.

6. Press the Play button at the top center of the editor to run the scene. You will see that the scene starts running and that balls are being dropped, but the balls just fall off the platforms. This is because the scene starts up in **Player** mode, which means you can control the platforms with keyboard input. Try to balance the balls on the platform using the arrow keys on the keyboard.

7. When you are done running the scene, click the Play button again to stop the scene.

Setting the agent Brain

As you witnessed, the scene is currently set for Player control, but obviously we want to see how some of this ML-Agents stuff works. In order to do that, we need to change the Brain type the agent is using. Follow along to switch the Brain type in the 3D Ball agent:

1. Locate the `Ball3DAcademy` object in the **Hierarchy** window and expand it to reveal the **Ball3DBrain** object.

2. Select the **Ball3DBrain** object and then look to the **Inspector** window, as shown in the following screenshot:

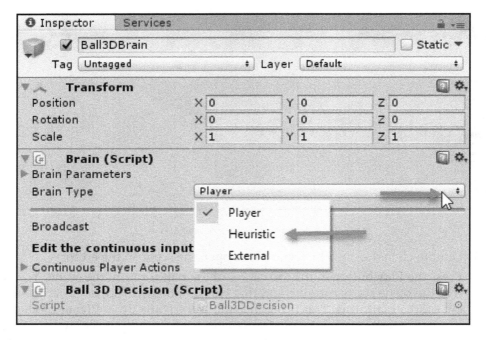

Switching the Brain on the Ball3DBrain object

3. Switch the Brain component, as shown in the preceding excerpt, to the **Heuristic** setting. The **Heuristic** brain setting is for **ML-Agents** that are internally coded within Unity scripts in a heuristic manner. Heuristic programming is nothing more than selecting a simpler quicker solution when a classic, in our case, ML algorithms, may take longer. Writing a Heuristic brain can often help you better define a problem and it is a technique we will use later in this chapter. The majority of current game AIs fall within the category of using Heuristic algorithms.

4. Press Play to run the scene. Now, you will see the platforms balancing each of the balls – very impressive for a heuristic algorithm. Next, we want to open the script with the heuristic brain and take a look at some of the code.

You may need to adjust the Rotation Speed property, up or down, on the **Ball 3D Decision (Script)**. Try a value of .5 for a rotation speed if the Heuristics brain seems unable to effectively balance the balls. The Rotation Speed is hidden in the preceding screen excerpt.

5. Click the Gear icon beside the **Ball 3D Decision (Script)**, and from the context menu, select **Edit Script**, as shown in the following screenshot:

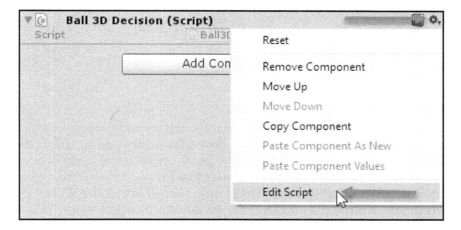

Editing the Ball 3D Decision script

6. Take a look at the Decide method in the script as follows:

```
public float[] Decide(
      List<float> vectorObs,
      List<Texture2D> visualObs,
      float reward,
      bool done,
      List<float> memory)
{
      if
      (gameObject.GetComponent<Brain()
      .brainParameters.vectorActionSpaceType
         == SpaceType.continuous)
      {
          List<float> act = new List<float>();
```

```
// state[5] is the velocity of the ball in the x orientation.
// We use this number to control the Platform's z axis rotation
 speed,
// so that the Platform is tilted in the x orientation
correspondingly.
  act.Add(vectorObs[5] * rotationSpeed);

// state[7] is the velocity of the ball in the z orientation.
// We use this number to control the Platform's x axis rotation
speed,
// so that the Platform is tilted in the z orientation
correspondingly.
  act.Add(-vectorObs[7] * rotationSpeed);

return act.ToArray();
}

// If the vector action space type is discrete, then we don't do
anything.
return new float[1] { 1f };
}
```

7. We will cover more details about what the inputs and outputs of this method mean later. For now though, look at how simple the code is. This is the heuristic brain that is balancing the balls on the platform, which is fairly impressive when you see the code. The question that may just hit you is: why are we bothering with ML programming, then? The simple answer is that the 3D ball problem is deceptively simple and can be easily modeled with eight states. Take a look at the code again and you can see that only eight states are used (0 to 7), with each state representing the direction the ball is moving in. As you can see, this works well for this problem but when we get to more complex examples, we may have millions upon billions of states – hardly anything we could easily solve using heuristic methods.

Heuristic brains should not be confused with **Internal** brains, which we will get to in Chapter 6, *Terrarium Revisited – Building a Multi-Agent Ecosystem*. While you could replace the heuristic code in the 3D ball example with an ML algorithm, that is not the best practice for running an advanced ML such as Deep Learning algorithms, which we will discover in Chapter 3, *Deep Reinforcement Learning with Python*.

In the next section, we are going to modify the Basic example in order to get a better feel for how ML-Agents components work together.

Creating an environment

One thing you may have noticed while looking over the last example was that an ML-Agent environment requires a bit of custom setup. Unity documentation recommends that an ML environment be constructed of Academy, Agent, and Brain objects with associated scripts. There is a Template folder in the ML-Agents project which we will use to configure and set up a simple environment. Let's jump back to the Unity editor and get started setting up our first simple ML environment:

1. Locate the `Template` folder in the `ML-Agents` folder within the **Project** window of the editor.
2. Right-click (*Command* Click on macOS) on the `Template` folder and select **Show in Explorer** from the context menu. This will open an **explorer** window with the files.
3. Select and copy the `Template` folder.
4. Navigate up two levels to the `Assets` folder and paste the copied folder. This will add the `Template` folder to the root `Assets` folder.
5. Rename the `Template` folder to `Simple`.

When you return to the editor, you will see a few namespace errors due to the duplicate Template scripts. We will fix that shortly.

6. Return to the Unity editor and confirm the folder and files have been copied to the new `Simple` folder, as shown in the following screenshot:

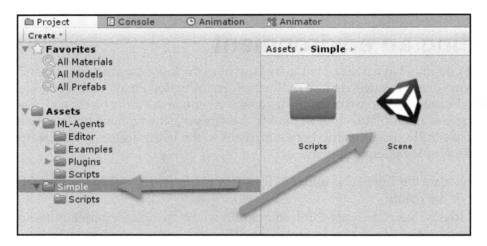

Verifying that the Simple folder was created

7. Double-click on the **Scene** to open it in the editor.

Renaming the scripts

That sets up the simple scene, but you may have noticed that there are still a few duplicated naming errors. We will need to rename the Template scripts in the `Simple/Scripts` folder. Follow this next exercise to rename each of the scripts:

1. Open the `Scripts` folder.
2. Rename each of the files from `Template` to `Simple`, as shown in the following excerpt of the **Project** window:

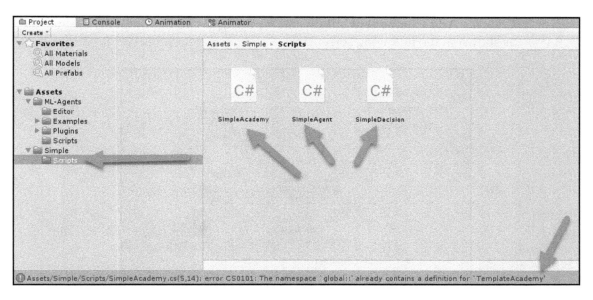

Renaming the Template scripts to Simple

3. Double-click on of the `SimpleAcademy` script file to open it in your code editor. Rename the class from `TemplateAcademy` to `SimpleAcademy` so that it matches the file name, as shown in the following code:

```
public class SimpleAcademy : Academy {
```

4. Repeat this process for the Agent and Decision scripts. The objects in the scene are still pointing to the template scripts, so we will update that next. Make sure to save all the scripts with your changes before returning to the editor. If all the files are renamed correctly, the naming errors will go away.

5. Select and rename the **Ball3DAcademy** to just `Academy` in the **Hierarchy** window.

6. Select the `Academy` object in the **Hierarchy** window. Click the Gear icon beside the `TemplateAcademy` component in the **Inspector** window and select **Remove Component** to remove the script.

7. Click the **Add Component** button and type `Simple` in the component search bar, as shown in the following screenshot:

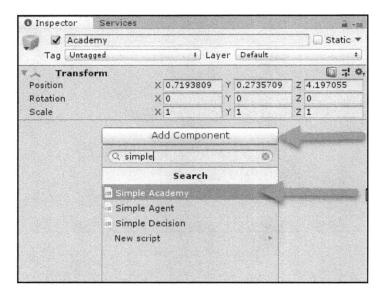

Adding the SimpleAcademy object to the Academy object

8. Click on the **Simple Academy** item, as shown in the preceding excerpt, to add the component to the `Academy` object.
9. Repeat the process for the `Agent` object and remove the `TemplateAgent` script and add the `SimpleAgent` script.
10. After you are done, be sure to save the scene and the project.

It is surprising that Unity didn't provide a better set of editor tools to build a new ML Agent environment, at least not at the time of writing this book. In the source code download for this book (`Chapter_1/Editor_Tools`), an asset package has been provided that can automate this setup for you. We may decide to put this package and some others from this book on the asset store.

That sets up a new ML environment for us to start implementing our own Academy, Agent, and Decision (Brain) scripts. We will get into the details of these scripts in the next section when we set up our first learning problem.

Academy, Agent, and Brain

In order to demonstrate the concepts of each of the main components (Academy, Agent, and Brain/Decision), we will construct a simple example based on the classic multi-armed bandit problem. The bandit problem is so named because of its similarity to the slot machine that is colloquially known in Vegas as the one armed bandit. It is named as such because the machines are notorious for taking the poor tourist's money who play them. While a traditional slot machine has only one arm, our example will feature four arms or actions a player can take, with each action providing the player with a given reward. Open up Unity to the **Simple** project we started in the last section:

1. From the menu, select **GameObject** | **3D Object** | **Cube** and rename the new object `Bandit`.
2. Click the Gear icon beside the **Transform** component and select **Reset** from the context menu. This will reset our object to (0,0,0), which works well since it is the center of our scene.
3. Expand the **Materials** section on the **Mesh Renderer** component and click the Target icon. Select the **NetMat** material, as shown in the following screenshot:

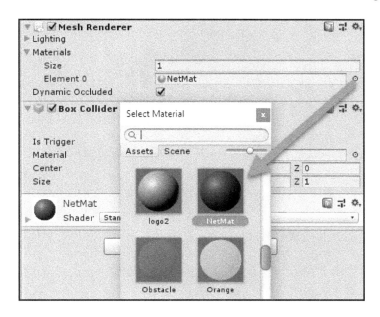

Selecting the NetMat material for the Bandit

4. Open the `Assets/Simple/Scripts` folder in the **Project** window.
5. Right-click (*Command* Click on macOS) in a blank area of the window and from the **Context** menu, select **Create** | **C# Script**. Name the script `Bandit` and replace the code with the following:

```
public class Bandit : MonoBehaviour
{
  public Material Gold;
  public Material Silver;
  public Material Bronze;
  private MeshRenderer mesh;
  private Material reset;

  // Use this for initialization
  void Start () {
  mesh = GetComponent<MeshRenderer>();
  reset = mesh.material;
  }

  public int PullArm(int arm)
  {
   var reward = 0;
   switch (arm)
    {
     case 1:
       mesh.material = Gold;
       reward = 3;
       break;
      case 2:
        mesh.material = Bronze;
        reward = 1;
        break;
      case 3:
       mesh.material = Bronze;
       reward = 1;
       break;
     case 4:
       mesh.material = Silver;
       reward = 2;
       break;
    }
    return reward;
  }

  public void Reset()
  {
    mesh.material = reset;
```

```
        }
    }
```

6. This code just simply implements our four armed bandit. The first part declares the class as **Bandit** extended from `MonoBehaviour`. All **GameObjects** in Unity are extended from `MonoBehaviour`. Next, we define some **public** properties that define the material we will use to display the reward value back to us. Then, we have a couple of **private** fields that are placeholders for the `MeshRenderer` called **mesh** and the original **Material** we call **reset**.

   We will implement the **Start** method next, which is a default Unity method that runs when the object starts up. This is where we will set our two private fields based on the object's `MeshRenderer`. Next comes the **PullArm** method which is just a simple switch statement that sets the appropriate material and reward. Finally, we will finish up with the **Reset** method where we just reset the original property.

7. When you are done entering the code, be sure to save the file and return to Unity.

8. Drag and drop the **Bandit** script from the `Assets/Simple/Scripts` folder in the **Project** window and drop it on the `Bandit` object in the **Hierarchy** window. This will add the **Bandit** component to the object.

9. Select the **Bandit** object in the **Hierarchy** window and then in the **Inspector** window click the **Target** icon and select each of the material slots (**Gold, Silver, Bronze**), as shown in the following screenshot:

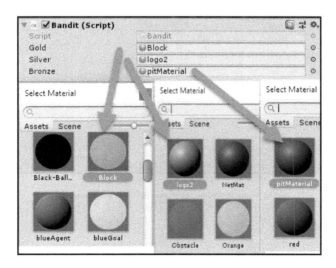

Setting the Gold, Silver and Bronze materials on the Bandit

This will set up our **Bandit** object as a visual placeholder. You could, of course, add the arms and make it look more visually like a multi-armed slot machine, but for our purposes, the current object will work fine. Remember that our **Bandit** has 4 arms, each with a different reward.

Setting up the Academy

An **Academy** object and component represents the training environment where we define the training configuration for our agents. You can think of an Academy as the school or classroom in which our agents will be trained. Open up the Unity editor and select the **Academy** object in the **Hierarchy** window. Then, follow these steps to configure the **Academy** component:

1. Set the properties for the **Academy** component, as shown in the following screenshot:

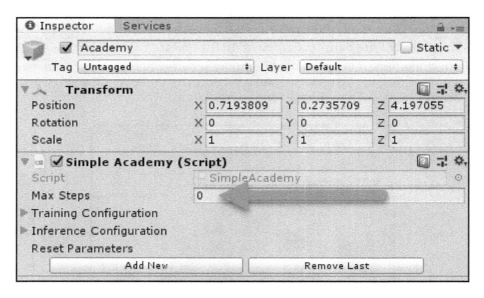

Setting the properties on the Academy component of the Academy object

2. The following is a quick summary of the initial **Academy** properties we will cover:

   - **Max Steps**: This limits the number of actions your **Academy** will let each **Agent** execute before resetting itself. In our current example, we can leave this at 0, because we are only doing a single step. By setting it to zero, our agent will continue forever until **Done** is called.
   - **Training Configuration**: In any ML problem, we often break the problem into a training and test set. This allows us to build an ML or agent model on a training environment or dataset. Then, we can take the trained ML and exercise it on a real dataset using inference. The *Training configuration* section is where we will configure the environment for training.
   - **Infrerence Configuration**: Inference is where we infer or exercise our model against a previously unseen environment or dataset. This configuration area is where we set parameters when our ML is running in this type of environment.

The **Academy** setup is quite straightforward for this simple example. We will get to the more complex options in later chapters, but do feel free to expand the options and look at the properties.

Setting up the Agent

Agents represents the actors that we are training to learn to perform some task or set of task-based commands on some reward. We will cover more about actors, actions, state, and rewards when we talk more about Reinforcement Learning in `Chapter 2`, *The Bandit and Reinforcement Learning*. For now, all we need to do is set the **Brain** the agent will be using. Open up the editor and follow these steps:

1. Locate the **Agent** object in the **Hierarchy** window and select it.

2. Click the **Target** icon beside the **Brain** property on the **Simple Agent** component and select the Brain object in the scene, as shown in the following screenshot:

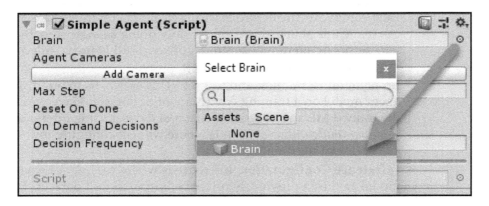

Setting the Agent Brain

3. Click the **Target** icon on the **Simple Agent** component and from the context menu select **Edit Script**. The agent script is what we use to observe the environment and collect observations. In our current example, we always assume that there is no previous observation.

4. Enter the highlighted code in the CollectObservations method as follows:

```
public override void CollectObservations()
{
    AddVectorObs(0);
}
```

5. CollectObservations is the method called to set what the **Agent** observes about the environment. This method will be called on every agent step or action. We use AddVectorObs to add a single float value of **0** to the agent's observation collection. At this point, we are not currently using any observations and will assume our bandit provides no visual clues as to what arm to pull.
The agent will also need to evaluate the rewards and when they are collected. We will need to add four slots, one for each arm to our agent, in order to represent the reward when that arm is pulled.

6. Enter the following code in the `SimpleAgent` class:

```
public Bandit bandit;
public override void AgentAction(float[] vectorAction,
string textAction)
{
  var action = (int)vectorAction[0];
  AddReward(bandit.PullArm(action));
  Done();
}

public override void AgentReset()
{
  bandit.Reset();
}
```

7. The code in our `AgentStep` method just takes the current action and applies that to the **Bandit** with the `PullArm` method, passing in the arm to pull. The reward returned from the bandit is added using `AddReward`. After that, we implement some code in the `AgentReset` method. This code just resets the Bandit back to its starting state. `AgentReset` is called when the agent is done, complete, or runs out of steps. Notice how we call the method **Done** after each step; this is because our bandit is only a single state or action.

8. Add the following code just below the last section:

```
public Academy academy;
public float timeBetweenDecisionsAtInference;
private float timeSinceDecision;

public void FixedUpdate()
{
  WaitTimeInference();
}

private void WaitTimeInference()
{
  if (!academy.GetIsInference())
  {
    RequestDecision();
  }
  else
  {
    if (timeSinceDecision >= timeBetweenDecisionsAtInference)
    {
      timeSinceDecision = 0f;
      RequestDecision();
```

```
      }
      else
      {
         timeSinceDecision += Time.fixedDeltaTime;
      }
   }
}
```

9. We need to add the preceding code in order for our brain to wait long enough for it to accept Player decisions. Our first example that we will build will use player input. Don't worry too much about this code, as we only need it to allow for player input. When we develop our Agent Brains, we won't need to put a delay in.

10. Save the script when you are done editing.

11. Return to the editor and set the properties on the Simple Agent, as shown in the following screenshot:

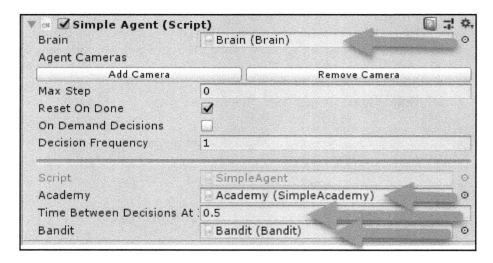

Setting the Simple Agent properties

We are almost done. The agent is now able to interpret our actions and execute them on the **Bandit**. Actions are sent to the agent from the **Brain**. The **Brain** is responsible for making decisions and we will cover its setup in the next section.

Setting up the Brain

We have seen the basics of how a `Brain` functions when we looked at the earlier Unity example. There are a number of different types of brains from **Player**, **Heuristic**, **Internal**, and **External**. For our simple example, we are going to set up a `Player` brain. Follow these steps to configure the **Brain** object to accept input from the player:

1. Locate the `Brain` object in the `Hierarchy` window; it is a child of the `Academy`.
2. Select the `Brain` object and set the `Player` inputs, as shown in the following screenshot:

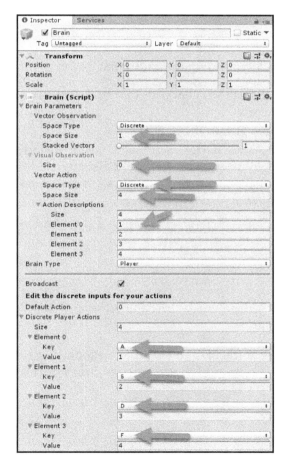

Setting the Player inputs on the Brain

3. Save your scene and project.

4. Press Play to run the scene. Type any of the keys *A*, *S*, *D*, or *F* to pull each of the arms from 1 to 4. As you pull the arm, the **Bandit** will change color based on the reward. This is a very simple game and a human pulling the right arm each time should be a fairly simple exercise.

Now, we have a simple **Player** brain that lets us test our simple four armed bandit. We could take this a step further and implement a **Heuristic** brain, but we will leave that as an exercise to the reader. For now though, until we get to the next chapter, you should have enough to run with to get comfortable with some of the basic concepts of ML-Agents.

Exercises

Complete these exercises on your own for additional learning:

1. Change the materials the agent uses to signal a reward – bonus points if you create a new material.

2. Add an additional arm to the Bandit.

3. In our earlier cannon example, we used a Linear Regression ML algorithm to predict the velocity needed for a specific distance. As we saw, our cannon problem could be better fit with another algorithm. Can you pick a better method to do this regression?

Access to **Excel** can make this fairly simple.

4. Implement a `SimpleDecision` script that uses a **Heuristic** algorithm to always pick the best solution.

You can look at the **3DBall** example we looked at earlier. You will need to add the `SimpleDecision` script to the **Brain** in order to set a Heuristics brain.

Summary

We covered the basics about Machine Learning and ML-Agents in this chapter by starting to introduce Machine Learning and the more common learning models, including Reinforcement Learning. After that, we looked at a game example with a cannon, where simple ML can be applied to solve the velocity required to strike a specific distance. Next, we quickly introduced ML-Agents and pulled the required code down from GitHub. This allowed us to run one of the more interesting examples in this book and explore the inner workings of the Heuristics brain. Then, we laid the foundations for a simple scene and set up the environment we will use over the next couple of chapters. Finally, we completed the chapter by setting up a simple Academy, Agent, and Brain, which were used to operate a multi-armed bandit using a Player brain.

In the next chapter, we will continue with our Bandit example and extend the problem to a contextual bandit, which is our first step toward Reinforcement Learning and building ML algorithms.

2
The Bandit and Reinforcement Learning

In the previous chapter, we introduced Machine Learning and the types of learning or training used in ML (Unsupervised Training, Supervised Training, Reinforcement Learning, Imitation Learning, and Curriculum Learning). As we discussed, the various forms of learning each have their own advantages and disadvantages. While ML using supervised training has been used successfully in games as far back as 20 years ago, it never really found any traction. It wasn't until the successful use of Reinforcement Learning was shown to be capable of playing classic Atari games and GO better than humans, that the interest for ML in games and simulations was rekindled. Now, RL is one of the hottest topics in ML research and is showing the potential for building some real continually learning AI. We will spend the bulk of this chapter understanding RL and how it can be applied to games and simulations with ML-Agents.

Reinforcement Learning and other forms of advanced learning are not without their criticism and, in general, are not trivial to setup. Keep this in mind as you progress through this book and then eventually build ML or brains on your own. Many critics of RL cite the difficulty of setup and configuration of hyperparameters, which is why we will explore several different helpful strategies to overcome these issues. Unity ML-Agents incorporate several of these strategies by default, and we will explore those later in this book as well.

In this chapter, we will explore many aspects of RL and other related principles such as contextual bandits. Here is a summary of the main topics we will cover in this chapter:

- Reinforcement Learning
- Contextual bandits and state
- Exploration and exploitation
- MDP and the Bellman equation
- Q-learning and connected bandits
- Exercises

If you missed the first chapter, be sure to download this book's source code, and load the asset package for Chapter_1_End. You will first need to pull the ML-Agents' code from GitHub, and the steps for this can be found in Chapter 1, *Introducing Machine Learning and ML-Agents*.

Reinforcement Learning

Reinforcement Learning is rooted in animal and behavioral psychology, where it is used in many applications of Machine Learning, from games and simulations to control optimization, information theory, statistics, and many more areas every day. RL, at its most basic level, describes an agent acting with an environment that receives either positive or negative rewards based on those actions. The following is a diagram showing the stateless RL model:

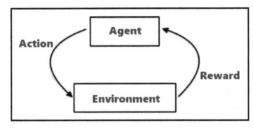

Stateless Reinforcement Learning

Conveniently, our multi-armed bandit problem we built in the last chapter fits well with this simpler form of RL. That problem only had a single state, or what we refer to as a one-step RL problem. Since the agent doesn't need to worry about state, we can greatly simplify our RL equations to just write the value of each action using the following equation:

$$V(a) = V(a) + \alpha \times (r - V(a))$$

Consider the following:

- $V(a) =$ A vector of values for each action (for example, 1.2, 2.2, 3, 4)
- $a =$ The action
- $\alpha =$ The learning rate, valued from 0 to 1. A value of 0 means no learning, whereas a higher value increases the rate of learning

- r =The reward observed for the action

The equation we have here is known as a *Value* function, and we use it to determine the value of an agent's actions. It is useful to understand how this equation works, so let's add the value function to our earlier bandit problem by following this exercise:

1. Open up the Unity editor to where we left off in the last chapter. Make sure that the **Bandit** is running correctly, using the **Player** brain.

    If you skipped the last chapter, you can access the code for Chapter01, in the Chapter_1_End.unitypackag from this book's source code folder. After the package has loaded, be sure to test the project, to make sure everything is working. You may need to reconfigure the Bandit object, so be sure the object has the Bandit script attached and that the Gold, Silver, and Bronze materials are set.

2. Select the Brain object, and then, on the Brain component, set the **Brain Type** to **Heuristic**. Click the Add Component button, and search for the SimpleDecision script, and add it to the object.

3. Click the Gear icon beside the new component, and select **Edit Script**. Enter the following code in the script:

```
using System.Collections.Generic;
using UnityEngine;
public class SimpleDecision : MonoBehaviour, Decision
{
    private int action;
    private int lastAction;
    public float learningRate;
    public float[] values = new float[4];

    public float[] Decide(
        List<float> vectorObs,
        List<Texture2D> visualObs,
        float reward,
        bool done,
        List<float> memory)
    {
        lastAction = action-1;
        if (++action > 4) action = 1;
        if (lastAction > -1)
        {
         values[lastAction] = values[lastAction] + learningRate *
         (reward -
         values[lastAction]);
```

```
        }
        return new float[] { action };
    }

    public List<float> MakeMemory(
        List<float> vectorObs,
        List<Texture2D> visualObs,
        float reward,
        bool done,
        List<float> memory)
    {
        return new List<float>();
    }
}
```

4. The `SimpleDecision` script is where the action happens, and the `Decide` method is where we need to set our actions. In this example, we are just cycling through the arms and determining the value function for the arm pulls. Inside the `Decide` method, we first grab the brain's last action. Then, we use some simple looping code to increment the current action, and when the action is greater than 4, we reset it back to 1. This will make our agent now systematically cycle through the bandit arms.

   As each arm is pulled, we use the **reward** returned from the previous action to calculate a new value for our value function. We store these values in an array, conveniently called values. In `MakeMemory`, we will just return the same memory at this point. When you are done with your edits, save your file and return to the editor.

> Keep in mind that in this state we are not evaluating any state. Our agent is this example we try all actions in a repetitive manner and will run until we stop the simulation. We can almost run the sample; we just need to configure the agent's new parameters.

Configuring the Agent

Return to the Unity editor and follow these steps to configure the agent:

1. Select the `Brain` object in the **Hierarchy** window.
2. Set the **Simple Decision** component parameters, as shown in the following screenshot:

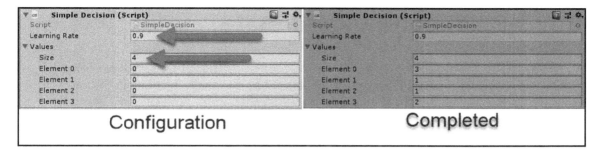

Agent configuration beside the agent running

3. After you enter the parameters, save the project and scene.
4. Press Play to run the scene, and with the `Brain` object selected, observe how the values for each action (0 for action 1) quickly converge to the `reward` values for each arm pull. The preceding screenshot also shows this. Remember that in the last chapter, we set these to the following:
   - `Arm 1 = Gold = 3 reward`
   - `Arms 2 and 3 = Bronze = 1 reward`
   - `Arm 4 = Silver = 2 reward`

If you encounter an observation error when running the simulation, don't worry; this sometimes occurs when reloading projects. Select the Brain object, and on the `Brain` component, delete all the camera observations. In other words, set the length to 0.

At this point, we are not making any decisions yet, but hopefully you can appreciate how useful it is to have a verifiable equation we can use to determine the value of an action. You could, of course, add some decision code to use the value function. That way, the brain could evaluate the next-best action and thus solve the multi-armed bandit problem... or could it? Think about it: After the agent's first action, arm pull 1, they will have receive a maximum reward of 3. At this point, the agent could stop after receiving the max reward, continue exploring, or keep pulling the same arm. This is known as the exploration/exploitation dilemma, and we will spend more time covering these questions and others in the next section on contextual bandits and state.

Contextual bandits and state

Our next step in understanding RL will be for us to look at the contextual bandit problem. A contextual bandit is the multi-armed bandit problem, with multiple bandits each producing different rewards. This type of problem has many applications in online advertising, where each user is thought of as a different bandit, with the goal being to present the best advertisement for that user. To model the context of the bandit, and which bandit it is, we add the concept of state. Where we now interpret state to represent each of our different bandits. The following diagram shows the addition of state in the Contextual Bandit problem and where it lies on our path to glory:

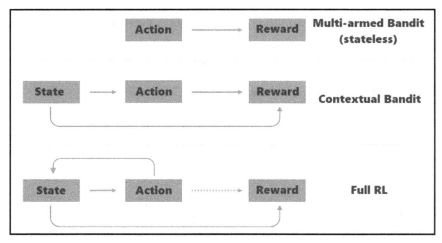

Stateless, Contextual and Full RL models

You can see in the preceding diagram that we now need to determine the state before evaluating an action. If you recall from earlier, the Value function only accepts an action, but now we also need to evaluate state. Let's rewrite our Value, or V, function to accept inputs of action and state as a function of Quality. We can rewrite our V function in terms of Quality as follows:

$$Q[s, a] = Q[s, a] + \alpha \times (r - Q[s, a])$$

Consider the follwing:

- $Q[s, a] =$Isa table or matrix of values. We denote the different by using $[\ ]$ instead of $(\ )$
- $s =$State

- a =Action
- α =The learning rate, valued from 0 to 1
- r =The reward observed for the state and action

This gives us the Quality, or Q, function which takes a state and action as input and returns the quality of a given action with a state or observation. While both Q and V functions are similar, the implementation in code within Unity is different and worth more careful discovery. Follow along as we covert the multi-armed bandit problem into a contextual bandit problem:

1. Open the `Assets/Simple/Scripts` folder in the `Project` window. Right-click (*Command* + click on macOS) in the window, and from the context menu, select `Create -> C# Script`.
2. Name the new script `SimpleArm`, and double click on it to open your code editor.
3. Simplify the script to just the following code:

```
using UnityEngine;

public class SimpleArm : MonoBehaviour {
    public Material material;
    public int rewardValue;
}
```

4. `SimpleArm` is a simple container for `Material` and `rewardValue`. Save the file when you are done editing.
5. Find the `Bandit` object in the `Hierarchy` window. Click the `Gear` icon beside the `Bandit` component in the `Inspector` window, and, from the context menu, select `Edit Script`.
6. Replace the **Gold**, **Silver**, and **Bronze Material** fields in the `Bandit.cs` script with the following code:

```
public SimpleArm[] arms;
```

7. We will use a `SimpleArm` array now, called `arms`.
8. Replace the entire contents of the `PullArm` method with the following code:

```
if (arm < 0 || arm > arms.Length) return 0;
mesh.material = arms[arm - 1].material;
return arms[arm-1].rewardValue;
```

9. As you can see, abstracting the arms like this greatly simplifies our `PullArm` method now. Save the file and return to Unity.

Now that we have the `Bandit.cs` and `SimpleArm.cs` scripts complete, we can go back to Unity and set up the game objects in the scene.

> Often, as you build up a scene, you may want to switch from deriving scripts or scene objects first. How you do this may depend on the problem you are tackling or just become a personal preference. Unity is great in that it allows you to construct those visual placeholders in the scene and then fill in the logic later.

Building the contextual bandits

Now, with the updated logic for the `Bandit` and `SimpleArm` classes, we can continue by configuring our scene objects. Follow these steps to create the multiple bandits:

1. From the menu, select `GameObject -> Create Empty`. Rename the new object `Arms`. We are going to make a container for all the bandit arms that the bandits will share. Sharing the arms will make setting up this task much simpler.
2. Select the new `Arms` object in the **Hierarchy** window, and then from the menu select `GameObject -> Create Empty`. This should create a new child object of `Arms`. Rename the new child object `GoldArm`.
3. Select `GoldArm`, and set its `Material` and `rewardValue` to one of your choosing.
4. With **GoldArm** selected, press *Ctrl + D(Command + D on* macOS)to duplicate the arm. Rename the new arm `SilverArm`, and adjust its properties appropriately.
5. Repeat step 4 for another arm called `BronzeArm`. You can create more arms at your own discretion. Try different materials and reward values as well.
6. Select the `Bandit` object, and in the **Inspector** window give the **Bandit** component four arms, as shown in the following screenshot:

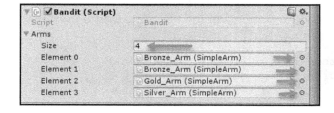

Setting up the Bandit arms

7. Select the **Bandit** object and type *Ctrl + D (Command + D on* macOS) to duplicate the bandit. Rename the object `Bandit_2`, and then reconfigure the arms any way you like, but be sure each bandit has four arms.
8. Repeat step 7 to add two more bandits named `Bandit_3` and `Bandit_4`. Be sure to reconfigure the arm positions for each bandit so they are different.
9. Set the **Transform Position X** of each bandit so they line up in a row with space between each bandit.
10. When you are done, save the scene and project.

After you are done, you should now have four bandits with four arms each, which gives us a Q function that represents a 4 X 4 table of state, action values. If you recall, we placed the V function in the `SimpleDecision`, and that means we will have to update the decision code next.

Creating the ContextualDecision script

We now need to upgrade the decision code from the multi-armed bandit problem to a contextual bandit problem. Go ahead and jump into the editor and follow these steps:

1. Locate the `SimpleDecision` script in the `Assets/Simple/Scripts` folder. Select the script and type *Ctrl + D (Command + D on macOS)* to duplicate the script. This will duplicate the script and cause an error. Not to worry; the error is just a duplicate name that we will fix shortly.
2. Rename the new script `ContextualDecision`, and then double-click on it to open it in your code editor.
3. Rename the class to `ContextualDecision` as follows:

```
public class ContextualDecision : MonoBehaviour, Decision
```

4. Add or modify the variable declarations at the top of the script as follows:

```
private int action;
private int lastAction, lastState;
public float[][] q;
public float learningRate;
```

5. Next, we will add a new `Awake` method to initialize our q table as follows:

```
public void Awake()
{
  q = new float[4][];
  for (int i = 0; i < 4; i++)
  {
    q[i] = new float[4];
  }
}
```

6. The `Decide` method also needs to be updated to the following:

```
public float[] Decide(
  List<float> vectorObs,
  List<Texture2D> visualObs,
  float reward,
  bool done,
  List<float> memory)
{
  lastAction = action-1;
  if (++action > 4) action = 1;
  if (lastAction > -1)
  {
    q[lastState][lastAction] = q[lastState][lastAction] +
    learningRate * (reward          - q[lastState][lastAction]);
  }
    lastState = (int)vectorObs[0];
    return new float[] { action };
  }
}
```

7. Notice how we swapped out the `Value` function we used in the last example with the q function. Remember, the q or Q function tracks state as well as the action. Notice at the end we are saving the `vectorObs[0]` value as our state. An observation is the same as capturing or observing state. Our state in this example will represent the current bandit that the agent is pulling the arm for.

8. Make sure to save the script and return to the editor. Just make sure you have no compile errors before continuing. Next, we need to replace the decision script on the Brain.

9. Locate the `Brain` object in the `Hierarchy` window and select it. Move to the `Inspector` window, and replace the `Simple Decision` component with the `Context Decision` component.

You have already swapped some components/scripts back in the first chapter. Be sure to also set the `learningRate` on the `Contextual Decision` component to a value of `.9`, again, just as we did in the last example.

That finishes up the new `ContextDecision` script, and now we can proceed to updating the agent script.

Updating the Agent

We are almost done. The last thing we need to do is set up the agent to be aware of the bandits and also return an observation for the current bandit. Open up the `SimpleAgent` script in your editor, and follow these steps to update the script:

1. Replace the following field declarations as follows:

   ```
   public Bandit bandit; //delete me
   public Bandit currentBandit;
   public Bandit[] bandits;
   ```

2. Next, we need to update the `CollectObservations` method as follows:

   ```
   public override void CollectObservations()
   {
     var bandit = Random.Range(0, bandits.Length);
     currentBandit = bandits[bandit];
     AddVectorObs(bandit);
   }
   ```

3. Here, we are returning the observation of the state the current agent is in. We determine the state by randomly selecting a `bandit` index that we use to pick the `currentBandit` from the array of `bandits`. We return the observation or state by using the `AddVectorObs(bandit)` call.

4. Modify the `AgentAction` method as follows:

   ```
   public override void AgentAction(float[] vectorAction,
   string textAction)
   {
     int action = (int)vectorAction[0];
     AddReward(currentBandit.PullArm(action));
   }
   ```

5. In `AgentStep`, we are again extracting the action. Then, execute the action on the `currentBandit` and collect the reward.

6. Finally, we need to update the `AgentReset` method with the following:

```
public override void AgentReset()
{
   if(currentBandit) currentBandit.Reset();
}
```

7. We just want to make sure the `currentBandit` is set before we call `Reset`. When you are done editing, save the file and return to Unity.

8. Select the **Agent** object in the **Hierarchy** window and set the **Bandits** on the **Simple Agent** component, as shown in the following screenshot:

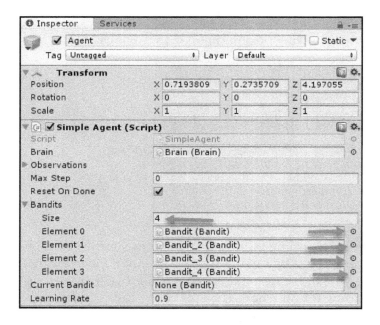

Setting the Bandits on the Agent

Our Agent is now configured, as shown in the previous screenshot. We now need to update the **Brain** and `SimpleDecision` script with a method or algorithm that allows us to explore and yet still exploit the environment. We will cover exploration and exploitation in the next section.

Exploration and exploitation

One of the dilemmas we face in RL is the balance between exploring all possible actions and exploiting the best possible action. In the multi-armed bandit problem, our search space was small enough to do this with brute force, essentially just by pulling each arm one by one. However, in more complex problems, the number of states could exceed the number of atoms in the known universe. Yes, you read that correctly. In those cases, we need to establish a policy or method whereby we can balance the exploration and exploitation dilemma. There are a few ways in which we can do this, and the following are the most common ways you can approach this:

- **Greedy Optimistic**: The agent initially starts with high values in its q table. This forces the agent to explore all states at least once, since the agent otherwise always greedily chooses the best action.
- **Greedy with Noise**: For each step, we randomly add noise to the value estimates. The random noise will range between the optimal action value and the current value. This allows the action values to converge to an optimal value.
- **Epsilon-greedy**: In this case, we set a fixed or converging probability that the agent will randomly explore. At each step, we test to see if there is a chance that the agent randomly explores or just greedily picks the current best action.

We will use the **Epsilon-greedy** method of exploration/exploitation in this example, but you are encouraged to build and try the other two options. In the next section, we will look at adding this form of exploration.

Making decisions with SimpleDecision

We have neglected to add any decision logic in our multi-armed bandit problem to keep things simple. Now that we have a better grasp of RL and the dilemma of exploration vs. exploitation, we can add the **Epsilon-greedy** exploration method. Epsilon-greedy exploration is a method whereby an agent's random chance of exploration decreases as the agent explores over time. This allows the agent to explore often early on, but as the agent learns, its chance of a random action decreases. Open the `ContextualDecision` script in your code editor and follow these steps:

1. Add the following `using` statement to the top of the file:

    ```
    using System.Linq;
    ```

2. Add the epsilon exploration field to the class, with the following declaration:

```
public float explorationEpsilon;
```

3. The `explorationEpsilon` field will be used to determine how probable it is that the brain/decision wants to explore, where this threshold value determines how randomly the agent will want to search. It is the epsilon in our `Epsilon-greedy` method. We will set it to a value from `0` to `1.0` when we train our brain later.

4. Modify the last line of the `Decide` method as follows:

```
return new float[] { action }; //replace this line
return DecideAction(q[lastState].ToList());
```

5. Add the new method `DecideAction` with the following code:

```
public float[] DecideAction(List<float> state)
{
  var r = Random.Range(0.0f, 1.0f);
  explorationEpsilon = Mathf.Min(explorationEpsilon-.001,.1f);
  if(r < explorationEpsilon)
  {
    action = RandomAction(state) + 1;
  } else {
    action = GetAction(state) + 1;
  }
  return new float[] { action };
}
```

6. In `Decide`, we randomly generate a value from `0.0f` to `1.0f`. This value, `r`, is then compared against the `explorationEpsilon` variable. If `r` is less than `explorationEpsilon`, we randomly pick an action; otherwise, we call `GetAction` to return the action. Then, we return an array with the selected `action`, just as we did before. Notice how we are decreasing `explorationEpsilon` after every call to decide. Again, we do this as a way to encourage early exploration, but over time our expectation is that our agent will have learned enough about the environment to be able to make confident decisions. We will leave it up to you to add properties for the minimum `explorationEpsilon` value, as it is currently hard-coded to `.1f`, or for the rate of decrease, set at `.01f`.

7. Next, we will create the `RandomAction` method as follows:

```
private int RandomAction(List<float> states)
{
  return Random.Range(0, states.Count);
}
```

8. Then, create the `GetAction` method as follows:

```
private int GetAction(List<float> values)
{
  float maxValue = values.Max();
  return values.ToList().IndexOf(maxValue);
}
```

9. In `GetAction`, we first find the `maxValue` of all the states using `Linq`. Then, we return the index position of the `maxValue`, which also happens to be our **action** index. This is the greedy method of picking the best action by selecting the one with the highest reward.

10. Leave `MakeMemory` as it is and save the file before returning to Unity.

11. Select the **Brain** underneath the **Academy** and configure it, as shown in the following screenshot:

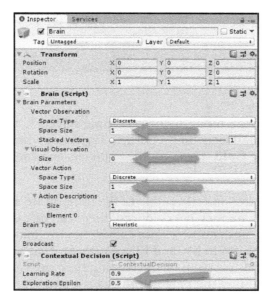

Setting the Brain configuration

12. We will use a high initial value for **Exploration Epsilon** of .5. This will allow us to watch our agent explore more. Save the scene and project.

13. Press **Play** to run the project and watch as the agent explores pulling arms. At some point, you should see your highest reward arm (Gold, in our example) appear more frequently.

14. Wait for a few seconds, or at most a minute, and your agent should have each of your bandits at the maximum reward showing the highlighted material. Now, sometimes, your agent may get so busy pulling the arms of other bandits that it may miss one bandit and you will see it get stuck on a bronze or silver arm, as shown in the following screenshot:

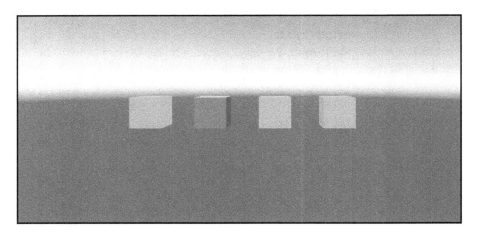

An Agent that has learned to maximize the Bandit rewards

15. See whether you can replicate the preceding screenshot by modifying the **Brain** object's **ContextualDecision** properties. Try to see what works to get all the **Bandits** showing **Gold**. Then, try the opposite, and see how badly you can make the agent run.

Now you should have a better understanding of the importance and some of the trade-offs with exploration in RL. As you may have noticed, there can be a delicate balance between how much your agent explores and how false confidence can make them blind. False confidence can be a big problem in ML and RL as a whole. Data scientists and other ML practitioner shave solved this problem by developing their own algorithm against a training dataset and then testing their algorithm against an unseen test or inference dataset. In ML-Agents, we will do all of our training using the training environment. You can do further training later with the inference environment on your own.

The learning rate and the exploration epsilon parameters we just played with would be classified as hyperparameters. These parameters often need to be adjusted for our brain or ML algorithm to learn the best global solution. In some cases, like we saw earlier, picking bad values for these parameters may only find a local optimum solution.

In the previous exercise, we introduced the importance and balance of exploration to encourage our contextual RL agent to explore and make confident decisions. In the next section, we advance to the full RL problem and learn how to build an agent to tackle more complex problems.

MDP and the Bellman equation

If you have studied Reinforcement Learning previously, you may have already come across the term MDP, for the Markov Decision Process, and the Bellman equation. An MDP is defined as a discrete time stochastic control (https://en.wikipedia.org/wiki/Stochastic) process, but, put more simply, it is any process that makes decisions based on some amount of uncertainty combined with mathematics. This rather vague description still fits well with how we have been using RL to make decisions. In fact, we have been developing MDP processes all of this chapter, and you should be fairly comfortable with the concept now.

Up until now, we have only modeled the partial RL or one-step problem. Our observation of state was only for one step or action, which meant that the agent always received an immediate reward or punishment. In a full RL problem, an agent may need to take several actions before receiving a positive reward. To model this advanced or delayed reward, we have to use the Bellman equation, which is as follows:

$$Q(s, a) = r + \gamma \max_{a'} Q(s', a')$$

Consider the following:

- $r = reward$
- $\gamma = gamma \ (reward \ discount \ factor \ 0 - 1.0)$
- $\max_{a'} = maximum \ of \ all \ actions \ for \ state$

The Bellman equation is used to predict the maximum future reward. We can combine this with our previous Q function and derive the following equation:

$$Q_{t+1}(s_t, a_t) = Q_t(s_t, a_t) + \alpha(r_{t+1} + \gamma \max_a Q_t(s_{t+1}, a) - Q_t(s_{t+1}, a_t))$$

Remember this:

$\alpha = learning\ rate$

This yields a new Q-Learning equation that is not that much different than the equations we already used in the previous exercises. By adding the Bellman equation, we are now accounting for one step of future rewards and can notice the subtle changes made to the equation. In particular, this includes how the future state is being taken as an input into our Q function, which allows for the calculation of the next state's maximum reward. The equation basically works by setting value breadcrumbs for each state and action pair. The agent learns when these value breadcrumbs have maximized in value. The agent then uses those value breadcrumbs to navigate its way to maximum rewards. The following diagram shows a game area grid where an agent has already run through 100 iterations and determined a number of Values and Q values:

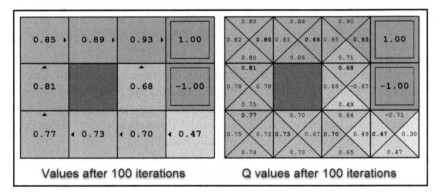

Value and Q values shown on a grid

The squares with values of 1.0 and -1.0 represent the final rewards for the ending squares, while all other squares have a reward value of -1. If you put a finger in any square on the grid and then just follow the direction the maximum Q value is pointing you in, you will find the path to the maximum reward, just as a Q-Learning agent would.

Is the path the agent takes optimal? Could it be better?

In the next section, we will demonstrate Q-Learning further by connecting our bandits together in an agent maze.

Q-Learning and connected agents

Typically, Q-Learning is taught using a grid problem such as the one we looked at it in the previous section. Here, though, we want something a little more complex and abstract that also allows you, the reader, to build on it and explore it further. We have put together an interesting example where we represent our bandits as rooms or objects with a number of exit options. This example could also very easily represent a dungeon or another connected room structure that you need to navigate an agent through. Follow these steps to get started on building the connected agents exercise:

1. From the menu, select `Assets -> Import Package -> Custom Package...`, then navigate to the book's downloaded source code and import the `Chapter_2_Connected_Bandits_unitypackage`. This is the example, which has been fully constructed already for you. Apologies in advance for those of you wanting more experience playing with Unity, but we want to dedicate as much time to ML as possible.

2. Import all the Assets and then open the **ConnectedBandits** scene that can be found in the `Assets/Simple` folder. After you open the scene, you should see something resembling the following screenshot:

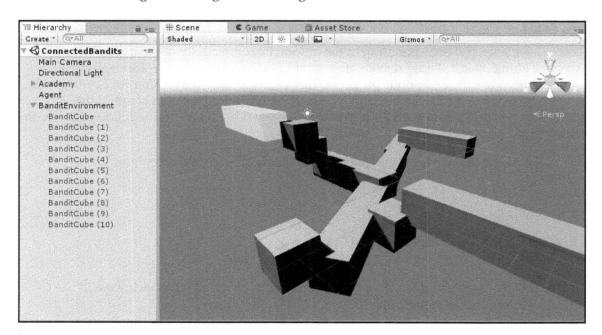

The ConnectBandits scene

3. Each cube or extended rectangle represents a room or connected object. The agent will be randomly dropped into one of the cubes and is then expected to make its way to the final **Gold** cube, which has a 1.0 reward. All the other cubes have a -.1 reward.

4. Press **Play** and let the scene run. You should see the agent, denoted by a blue material, occupy each of the cubes trying to finds its way to the end (**Gold** cube). Let the agent run for a while, and you should see it eventually get quite good at finding its way home. Stop the scene when you are happy with the agent's progress.

The maze is constructed using BanditCubes. These cubes are just objects set with colliders that allow the cubes to auto-detect other cubes they are touching. This will allow you to modify the maze on your own by adding new cubes by using *Ctrl+D* [*Command+D* on macOS] or moving cubes around in any manner. As long as the cubes are touching, the agent will have a path to follow. Feel free to make a super complex maze and see how long it takes to train your agent.

Looking at the Q-Learning ConnectedDecision script

There is some special code handling in the automatic connectivity of the cubes, but we won't be going over it. Those readers that want to extend this example are encouraged to explore the code further. For our purposes, however, the only main thing we need to look at is the changes in the Decision script. Locate the **ConnectedDecision** script in the Assets/Simple folder and double click on it to open it in your editor to follow along with these steps:

1. At the top, we have the following declarations:

```
public float learningRate = .9f;
public float gamma = .9f;
public float explorationEpsilon = .9f;
private float[][] q;
private int lastAction, lastState;
private int action;
```

2. You can see that we have introduced a new term, gamma, which we will use to discount the future reward.

3. Scroll down a little to the Q property or function:

```
public float[][] Q {
  get{
    if (q == null)
    {
       var connectedAcademy =
       Object.FindObjectOfType<ConnectedAcademy>() as
       ConnectedAcademy;
       q = new float[connectedAcademy.bandits.Length][];
       foreach(var bandit in connectedAcademy.bandits)
       {
         if (bandit.Connections.Count == 0)
         {
           q = null;
           return q;
         }
         q[bandit.index] = new float[bandit.Connections.Count];
       }
    }
    return q;
    }
}
```

4. We write Q as a property for convenience and handling. Inside, we set up the initial values based on the bandit connections. The ConnectedAcademy holds a reference to the BanditEnvironment, which is a container for BanditCubes. Notice how we are constructing a jagged array, since the number of connections for each bandit may vary.

 The Q-Learning equation we just derived is in the family of RL algorithms we will further explore in the coming chapters, as well as many other techniques for their use. We have only just begun our exploration of RL and other forms of learning, and we will explore more in later chapters.

5. Finally, the main change is in the Decide method, as you can see from this code:

```
public float[] Decide(List<float> vectorObs, List<Texture2D>
visualObs, float
reward, bool done,                     List<float> memory)
{
  if (Q == null) return new float[] { 0 };
  lastAction = action-1;
  var state = (int)vectorObs[0];
  if (lastAction > -1)
  {
```

```
        Q[lastState][lastAction] = Q[lastState][lastAction] +
        learningRate * (reward
        + gamma * Q[state].Max()) - Q[lastState][lastAction];
    }
    lastState = state;
    return DecideAction(Q[state].ToList());
}
```

6. We have covered most of the code already in the Decide method, so we won't need to go over it again. Just make sure and understand the differences with this Q function and the previous versions we looked at in the earlier exercises.

That covers most of the relevant code that we need to go over. As mentioned earlier, there are plenty of other code changes sprinkled around that were required to make this version run automatically. While you may find the other code interesting, it is not essential for our current journey in learning ML.

 The only other major change in the sample was setting the Max Steps on the Agent to 100 from 0. This tells the agent to move up to 100 steps before restarting, if it hasn't found the goal. You may need to adjust this higher if you build large, complex mazes. Remember that the agent may need to wander around for a while before they get useful breadcrumbs to follow.

Many courses on Reinforcement Learning spend more time covering the basics of MDP and the concept of maximizing rewards based on observed state. However, they often fail to cover the specific implementation details we just covered in explicit detail. Therefore, it is recommended that the reader watch one of the many free online lecture series on RL and MDP which have been provided by several accredited universities. You may also find that learning the complex maths that these courses go into is now more accessible now that you have learned the practical uses of those algorithms.

With the basics of RL out of the way, you should have a comfortable enough grasp to dig into more complex tasks in later chapters. For now, though, be sure to try the exercises in the next section on your own.

Exercises

"For the things we have to learn before we can do them, we learn by doing them."

– Aritstotle

Be sure to complete the following questions or exercises on your own:

1. Extend the bandit cube maze in the last section with your own design. Make sure to keep all the cubes connected so that the agent has a clear path to the end.
2. Think of another problem in gaming, simulation, or otherwise, where you could use RL and the Q-Learning algorithm to help an agent learn to solve this problem. This is just a thought exercise, but give yourself a huge pat on the back if you build a demo.
3. Add new properties for the Exploration Epsilon minimum and the amount of change per decision step. Remember, these are the parameters we hard-coded in order to decrease the epsilon-greedy exploration value.
4. Add the ability to show the Q values on the individual BanditCube objects. If you can view the values as properties, that works too. Be sure to show the Q value for each connection.
5. Explore one of the other Unity ML examples, and try your hand at developing a heuristic brain that uses the Q-Learning algorithm.

Summary

In this chapter, we dove into working with the ML-Agents framework by developing a heuristic brain that uses an ML technique called Reinforcement Learning to solve various fundamental learning problems. We first explored the classic multi-armed bandit problem in order to first introduce the concepts of RL. Then, we expanded on this problem by adding context or the sense of state. This required us to modify our Value function by adding state and turning our function into a Q function. While this algorithm worked well to solve our simple learning problem, it was not sufficient for more complex problems with delayed rewards. Introducing delayed rewards required us to look at the Bellman equation and understand how we could discount rewards over an agent's steps, thus providing the agent with Q value breadcrumbs as a way for it to find its way home. Finally, we loaded up a complex, connected bandit problem that requires our agent to navigate complex mazes using Q-Learning.

In the next chapter, we will take another leap in our learning of ML by introducing Python and a number of libraries that will give us some ML power tools. We will begin to explore these Python power tools in the next chapter.

Deep Reinforcement Learning with Python

3

Over the last couple of chapters, we learned about the basics of ML—and, of course, specifically RL—using the Unity editor, and things were good. Unfortunately, the number of states in an RL problem can quickly exceed billions. The number of states in the game Go has been calculated to exceed the number of atoms in the observable universe, for instance. Now, dealing with these unfathomable numbers of states and doing the math for these types of problems isn't trivial. In fact, it is only just recently that we have been able to grapple with these numbers, thanks to the efforts of Google and others in releasing some powerful ML tools collectively called TensorFlow. TensorFlow is a math-execution library that has become the cornerstone of ML research because of the power it provides. Now, the preferred toolset when working with TensorFlow is Python. Unity, not wanting to reinvent a massive wheel, decided to build ML-Agents around Python and TensorFlow. As such, in this chapter, we will learn how to set up Python and use those tools to develop more advanced ML agents.

In this chapter, we will dive into working with Python and a number of other ML tools and libraries. The following are the main areas that we will focus on in this chapter:

- Installing Python and tools
- The ML-Agent external brain
- Neural network foundations
- Deep Q-learning
- Proximal policy optimization

Python has become the preferred standard language/environment when working in ML. Honestly, with the number of free and powerful ML tools available for Python, it really doesn't make sense to work with any other language or platform.

Installing Python and tools

In this section, we will cover some of the basics of Python, but we do not have enough time to cover the language in depth. If you are new to Python but have plenty of programming experience with C#, you should be fine to proceed. For those of you with experience in Python, you may still want to pay special attention to the setup as, at the time of writing, ML-Agents is only supported by Python 3.5.

Python is a great language to learn if you are new to programming. However, for more experienced C# developers, it can be intimidating to learn a new language/framework that is outside the family, so to speak. After all, Python is more than a language: It is a multiple programming paradigm that also supports functional, aspect-orientated, and meta-programming. If you are not sure about learning a new language, do yourself a big favor and give Python a try—you may be more than pleasantly surprised.

Installation

Proceed with the relevant setup for your operating system, as shown in the following two recipes.

Mac/Linux installation

The following setup guide is provided as an overview of the guide that came with the Unity ML-Agents source we cloned in Chapter 1, *Introducing Machine Learning and ML-Agents*. We included this guide for the sake of completeness, but chances are that if you use Linux, you will likely already have Python installed. Go through the following steps to install Python and the tools:

1. Download and install Python 3 from https://www.python.org/downloads/.
2. Make sure pip is installed as well. If you're not sure, check https://packaging.python.org/guides/installing-using-linux-tools/#installing-pip-setuptools-wheel-with-linux-package-managers.
3. Navigate to the ML-Agents folder, which we cloned earlier.
4. Navigate to the python folder and type the following command:

```
pip3 install .
```

You should see the required dependencies get installed.

If you have any problems, be sure to consult the Unity docs for any special instructions. Overall, installing Python and the required dependencies on macOS/Linux is embarrassingly simple compared to installing them on Windows, which we will cover next.

Windows installation

The current version of Unity ML-Agents has only been found to work with Windows 10. You can try to use an earlier operating system, but expect to encounter issues. If you do, use the following guide to install the Python environment for ML-Agents:

1. Install Anaconda 3.6 (64-bit) from `https://www.anaconda.com/download/`.
2. Follow the instructions of the installer. Be sure to use the Advanced Options and set the PATH as shown in the following:

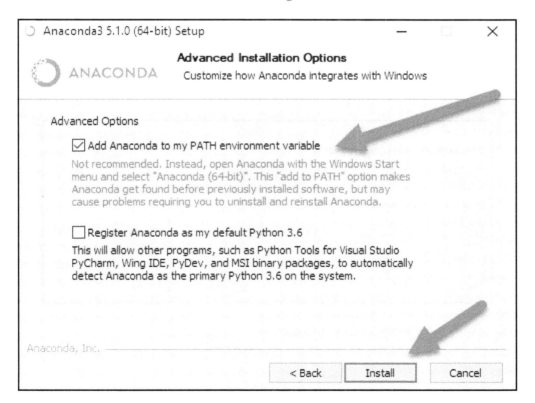

3. While this isn't recommended, setting this option will be useful for us in later sections of the book. Anaconda will prompt you to install Visual Studio Code after it has finished the installation. If you don't already have VS Code, be sure to select this option to download and install it as well. We will use VS Code in a later chapter of this book, and installing it now will save you a step later on.

4. Test the installation of Anaconda by launching Anaconda Navigator. Press the Windows key and then enter anaconda navigator to quickly find and launch the app. Leave the app open, as we will get back to it shortly.

5. Open a new Anaconda prompt by entering anaconda prompt in the search bar (press the Windows key).

6. Enter the following command in the prompt window:

```
conda create -n ml-agents python=3.5
```

7. This command will create a new 3.5 Python environment named [-n] ml-agents. Follow any prompts that require you to download dependencies, for which, of course, you will want to be connected to the internet. ML-Agents is currently dependent on Python 3.5; therefore, we need to explicitly state that we want to use Python 3.5.

8. Activate the environment by entering the following:

```
conda activate ml-agents
```

9. Install TensorFlow by running the following:

```
pip install tensorflow==1.4.0
```

10. This will install a number of required packages, but we still need a few more.

11. Navigate to the python folder in the ml-agents source folder. If you recall, we downloaded this to C:\ML-Agents\ml-agents\, if you followed the instructions for downloading the ML-Agents source from GitHub in Chapter01:

```
cd c:\ML-Agents\ml-agents\python
```

12. Install the required Python dependencies for ML-Agents by running the following:

```
pip install .
```

13. Double-check the folder before running the preceding command. Once the libraries are installed, your environment is done and you can move on.

If you run into problems, you can always run the entire installation again and just choose a different folder to install it into. You may also find it useful to set up a couple of different environments to run and test.

Docker installation

If you are familiar with Docker, this is also another great option. We won't cover the specific details of using Docker here, and you should consult the guide for your required operating system.

GPU installation

TensorFlow supports the use of a GPU for developing highly computational applications as if we were building with ML-Agents. While using a GPU is essential for numerically complex problems, ML-Agents does not currently require a supported GPU in order to run TensorFlow. This means that we can currently bypass installing the support for GPU drivers. If you want to use TensorFlow with a GPU, be sure to check Unity's internal docks and the proper setup guidelines for your hardware and operating system.

Testing the install

After you install Python and the required dependencies for your OS, make sure everything is installed correctly. Fortunately, the commands to run the tests are essentially the same for all OSes currently supported. Go through the following quick steps to test the installation:

1. Open a command shell or an Anaconda prompt window, as you did previously.
2. Navigate to the `ml-agents/python` folder. If you are continuing from the previous exercise, you should already be there.

3. Enter the following command in your shell or Anaconda prompt window:

```
jupyter notebook
```

4. This should open your default browser with the Jupyter Notebook window, as shown in the following screenshot:

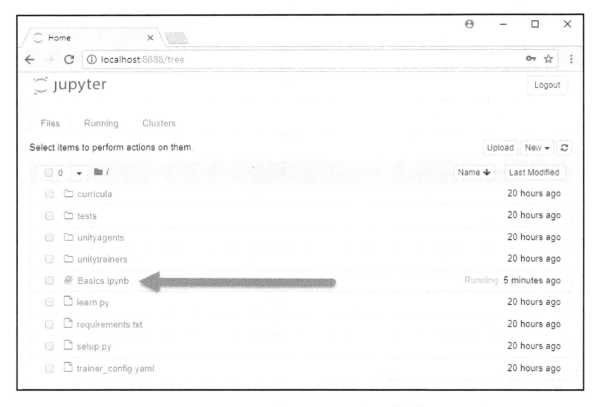

Jupyter Notebook running from the python folder

5. Click on the Basics.ipynb file, as shown in the preceding screenshot. If your browser doesn't open to the page, you can open a browser and enter http://localhost:8888 to access the page. If the page is showing something else, make sure you entered the address correctly and that some other service isn't using port 8888.

6. This will load the Basics notebook. Basics is an introductory test notebook that you can use to test the proper setup of the Unity test environment.

That is all we need to cover for now. We will jump into setting up your first ML-Agents external brain in the next section.

ML-Agents external brains

Until now, all of our experiments have been with the heuristics brain using an internal RL algorithm called Q-learning. Now that we realize that C# scripts will only go so far, we can look at using ML-Agent external brains developed with Python. The preferred method for Unity is to run a Jupyter Python notebook externally to control the Unity training environment. This requires us to build a special Unity environment. Go through the following steps to learn how to configure the 3D ball environment for external training:

1. Open the Unity editor and load the ML-Agents demo `unityenvironment` project. If you still have it open from the last chapter, then that will work as well.
2. Open the `3DBall.scene` in the `ML-Agents/Examples/3DBall` folder.
3. Locate the `Brain3DBrain` object in the **Hierarchy** window and select it. In the **Inspector** window set the Brain Type to External.
4. From the menu, select **Edit | Project Settings | Player**. From the **Inspector** window, set the properties as shown in the following screenshot:

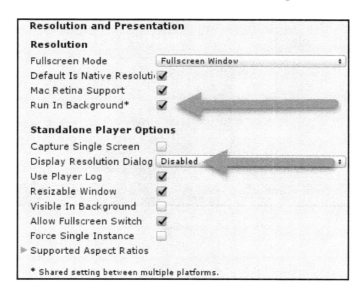

5. Setting the **Player** resolution properties
6. From the menu, select **File | Build Settings**. Click on the Add Open Scene button and make sure that only the **3DBall** scene is active, as shown in the following dialog:

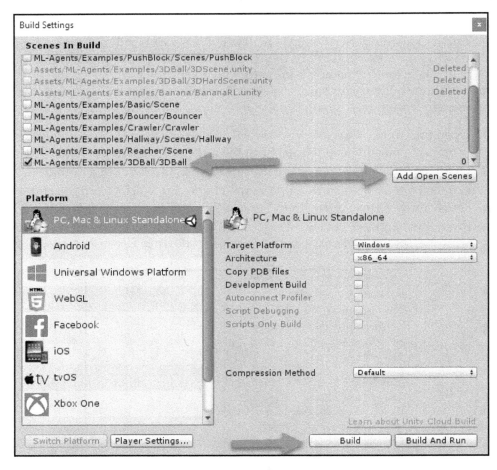

Setting the Build Settings for the Unity environment

7. Set the Target Platform to your chosen desktop OS (Windows, in this example) and click the Build button at the bottom of the dialog.

8. You will be prompted to choose a folder to build into. Select the python folder in the base of the ml-agents folder.

9. If you are prompted to enter a name for the file, enter 3DBall. On newer versions of Unity, from 2018 onward, the name of the folder will be set by the name of the Unity environment build folder, which will be python.
Be sure that you know where Unity is placing the build, and be sure that the file is in the python folder. At the time of writing, on Windows, Unity will name the executable `python.exe` and not `3DBall.exe`. This is important to remember when we get to setting up the Python notebook.

With the environment built, we can move on to running the Basics notebook against the app. In the next section, we will walk through running the Jupyter notebook to control the environment.

Running the environment

Open up the Basics Jupyter notebook again; remember that we wanted to leave it open after testing the Python install. If you have experience with Python and Jupyter, you may just want to read through the notebook on your own. For those of you that want a little more help, go through the following steps:

1. Ensure that you update the first code block with your environment name, like so:

```
env_name = "python" # Name of the Unity environment binary to launch
train_mode = True # Whether to run the environment in training or
inference mode
```

2. We have the environment name set to `'python'` here because that is the name of the executable that gets built into the python folder. You can include the file extension, but you don't have to. If you are not sure what the filename is, check the folder; it really will save you some frustration.

3. Go inside the first code block and then click the Run button on the toolbar. Clicking Run will run the block of code you currently have your cursor in. This is a really powerful feature of a notebook; being able to move back and forth between code blocks and execute what you need is very useful when building complex algorithms.

4. Click inside the second code block and click Run. The second code block is responsible for loading code dependencies. Note the following line in the second code block:

```
from unityagents import UnityEnvironment
```

5. This line is where we import the `unityagents` UnityEnvironment class. This class is our controller for running the environment.

6. Run the third code block. Note how a Unity window will launch, showing the environment. You should also notice an output showing a successful startup and the brain stats. If you encounter an error at this point, go back and ensure you have the `env_name` variable set with the correct filename.

7. Run the fourth code block. You should again see some more output, but unfortunately, with this control method you don't see interactive activity. We will try to resolve this issue in a later chapter.

8. Run the fifth code block. This will run through some random actions in order to generate some random output.

9. Finally, run the sixth code block. This will close the Unity environment.

Feel free to review the Basics notebook and play with the code. Take advantage of the ability to modify the code or make minor changes and quickly rerun code blocks. Don't concern yourself too much if the code looks complicated; there are plenty of good examples and we have plenty more chapters to go through.

At this point, you may still be scratching your head and asking "why Python?". Indeed, we could have just as easily written the same example quite cleanly in C#. Python provides us with an advanced set of algorithms developed explicitly for solving complex ML problems. One such algorithm or tool that we use is known as a neural network, and we will explore how we use it in the next section.

Neural network foundations

Neural networks provide the foundations for some of the most impressive AI/ML algorithms that we have seen in recent years. They have also become the cornerstone or standard for several areas of AI, from image and speech recognition to playing Atari games. This sounds really intimidating, but actually, a neural network is a quite a simple and elegant structure modeled after our own human brain. The foundation of our brain and nervous system is a single neuron, shown in the following image beside a simulated computer neuron:

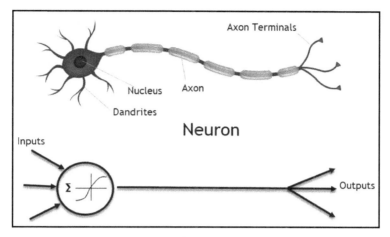

A neuron

The simulated neuron in the preceding diagram represents the structure of a single neuron. The inputs, or signals, into the neuron are typically summed and then evaluated against some form of activation function. You can see an example activation function in the diagram. When a neuron is activated, or fired, it sends out an output that can either be fed into more neurons or as a final output. The following image shows a multiple-layer neural network:

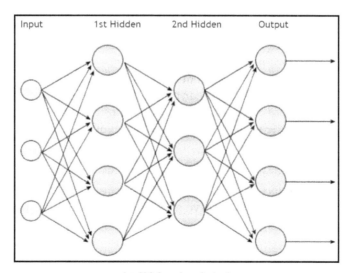

A multiple-layered neural network

The preceding diagram represents a typical simple neural network with an input and output and two hidden layers of neurons. We call the layers of neurons in between the input and output hidden because we don't typically interact with these layers. The final layer, the output layer, is where the network spits out the answer. At first, that answer is rubbish, because the network is untrained and has no sense of what a right answer should be. In order to be especially useful, a neural network needs to be trained as to what the right or perhaps wrong answer is. There are numerous ways to do this, but the more common way is to back-propagate the errors from the output back through the network.

Backwards propagation is a fundamental concept in neural networks and deep learning. It is a method whereby the activation function of each neuron gets weighted based on its contribution to the total amount of error. We generally do this in a very slow, iterative manner in order to find the best fit. This means that a typical neural network needs to be exposed to thousands of samples or iterations to develop effectively.

We don't have time to go into back propagation, gradient descent, and activation functions in any detail. It is recommended that you take an hour or so and learn these fundamentals when you have the time, perhaps between chapters. There are plenty of great resources online that can delve into the details of neural networks in any depth you need.

But what does it do?

At their core, neural networks are just really good, nonlinear function approximators, which means they are just good at solving equations. If you think back to our first example in Chapter 1, *Introducing Machine Learning and ML-Agents*, we used a simple linear ML algorithm called linear regression to predict cannon velocities. While we were able to estimate things reasonably well with a linear method, what we really needed was a nonlinear solution. While there are a variety of other nonlinear methods we could use, neural networks provide us the ability to develop more generalized and better-fitting solutions, without all the math.

For us, this means neural networks—or deep networks, as we will call them—will be used as a tool to solve our Q-learning equations and other more complex problems. We will look at how we can use a neural network to solve a Q-learning problem in the next section.

Deep Q-learning

Now that we understand some of the foundations of neural networks, it will be really helpful to look at a very basic example in Python that demonstrates their use. Go through the following steps to build a neural network that trains an agent with deep Q-learning. Windows users, make sure that you open an Anaconda prompt and switch to the `ml-agents` environment with `activate ml-agents`, as we did earlier.

1. Open a command prompt or shell window to an empty folder and enter the following:

    ```
    git clone https://github.com/matthiasplappert/keras-rl.git
    cd keras-rl
    python setup.py install
    ```

2. This will install Keras RL, the reinforcement learning package for Keras. Keras is a popular library for building neural networks and other ML tasks. It can be backed by TensorFlow or Theano. Since we already have TensorFlow installed, we are good.

3. Enter the following:

    ```
    pip install h5py
    pip install gym
    ```

4. The `h5py` code phrase is a Pythonic interface to the HDF5 format, and allows you to work with large numerical datasets. The next line installs `gym`, which is Python ML test environment.

5. Download and install Visual Studio Code. This will be our preferred Python editor, but feel free to use another IDE or editor of your preference if you are an experienced Python developer.

This will install all the required dependencies we will need for our quick example. Next, we will look at writing the Python code to build the example.

There are hundreds of examples that demonstrate Q-learning with Keras that are available on the internet, but many of the examples are quite complex, or provide complex stats code. The example we will look at here has been chosen because it is succinct and works quickly. Feel free to explore many of the other examples on your own.

Building the deep network

Normally, after introducing neural networks, we would start with a simple example of perhaps a single neuron or layer. However, that type of sample would be less than impressive, and is small fry compared to building a working deep Q-learning example. This means that in order to build a working example, we need to jump into the deep end, pun intended. Go through the following exercise to build the example:

1. Open Visual Studio Code, click **File** | **New File**, and create a new file named `DeepQLearning.py`.

2. This first part of the code imports the various libraries we need, enter the following code

   ```
   import numpy as np
   import gym

   from keras.models import Sequential
   from keras.layers import Dense, Activation, Flatten
   from keras.optimizers import Adam

   from rl.agents.dqn import DQNAgent
   from rl.policy import EpsGreedyQPolicy
   from rl.memory import SequentialMemory
   ```

3. Then we set up some base variables with the following:

   ```
   ENV_NAME = 'CartPole-v0'

   env = gym.make(ENV_NAME)
   np.random.seed(123)
   env.seed(123)
   nb_actions = env.action_space.n
   ```

4. We are going to use the cart–pole problem from the `gym` library, and this is why we set `ENV_NAME` to `CartPole-v0`. Then we create the `env` environment with `gym.make`. Once this is done, we create a random seed with a set seed value. This allows us to create a reproducible random sequence to allow us to reproduce results.

5. Next, we build the neural network with the following:

   ```
   model = Sequential()
   model.add(Flatten(input_shape=(1,) + env.observation_space.shape))
   model.add(Dense(16))
   model.add(Activation('relu'))
   ```

```
model.add(Dense(nb_actions))
model.add(Activation('linear'))
print(model.summary())
```

6. We start by creating a sequential network. A sequential network is an ordered stack of layers not unlike the image of the neural network we saw earlier. To build a sequential network, we add layers of neurons that will be connected to each other. The first layer we add is the input layer that is flattened with Flatten, meaning that it creates an input layer of neurons corresponding to the number of observations. Next, we create a normal Dense layer with 16 neurons using a relu activation function. Finally, we finish with another Dense output layer with a linear activation function.

   The model we are building is defined by the tensor shape of our input. In this case, that shape is a simple 1 x 4 array of inputs. The inputs into the model will be the observed state of the agent, with the final output representing the optimum action for the observed state.

7. Save the file. The relu, or ReLu, activation functions and other details can be found online at the Keras documentation site.

8. Debug the sample by selecting **Debug** | **Start Debugging** from the menu. This will run the code we have so far, and should output a summary of the model (neural network), as shown in the following code:

```
Layer (type) Output Shape Param #
=================================================================
flatten_1 (Flatten) (None, 4) 0

dense_1 (Dense) (None, 16) 80

activation_1 (Activation) (None, 16) 0

dense_2 (Dense) (None, 2) 34

activation_2 (Activation) (None, 2) 0
=================================================================
Total params: 114
Trainable params: 114
Non-trainable params: 0
```

Take a look at the output and you will see that we have built a 4-input, 16-hidden-layer, and 2-output neural network. This is a very simple network that we are going to use to fit our Q-learning equation. This means we don't have to write our equation, since we are using the NN to essentially work as our equation solver.

Training the model

In order for our neural network to fit our Q-learning equation, we need to train it iteratively, typically over thousands of iterations. We do this so that our model (network) can gradually fit the equation to our learning problem without getting stuck at a local minimum or maximum. The parameters we can adjust for training are numerous, and can be complex, but don't worry. Go through the following exercise to finish the sample and train the model:

1. Enter the following code just beneath the last section:

   ```
   policy = EpsGreedyQPolicy()
   memory = SequentialMemory(limit=50000, window_length=1)
   dqn = DQNAgent(model=model, nb_actions=nb_actions, memory=memory,
   nb_steps_warmup=10,
   target_model_update=1e-2, policy=policy)
   dqn.compile(Adam(lr=1e-3), metrics=['mae'])
   dqn.fit(env, nb_steps=5000, visualize=True, verbose=2)
   ```

2. We start by creating a policy of the `EpsGreedyQPolicy` type, which is just a variation of the epsilon greedy policy we have already been using. Next, we set up the memory using `SequentialMemory` with a limit of `50000`. This is where we will store the agents' observations of state for training. Next, we build a `DQNAgent` with the `nb_actions` model's memory and policy. This agent is essentially a brain (in Unity terms) that handles the input and training. Next, we compile the `dqn` with an Adam optimizer. Adam introduces a newer form of training rather than using the classic stochastic gradient descent. After that, we finish with a call to fit, which essentially runs the training on the `env` environment visually with `5000` steps.

3. Finish the script by entering the following:

   ```
   dqn.test(env, nb_episodes=5, visualize=True)
   ```

4. This last line will test the agent/brain in the environment.

5. Save the file.
6. Debug the script by clicking **Debug | Start Debugging**. After selecting the option in the menu, you may need to select your Python environment as well. As the script runs, you will see the gym environment displayed with the cart–pole problem running, as shown in the following screenshot:

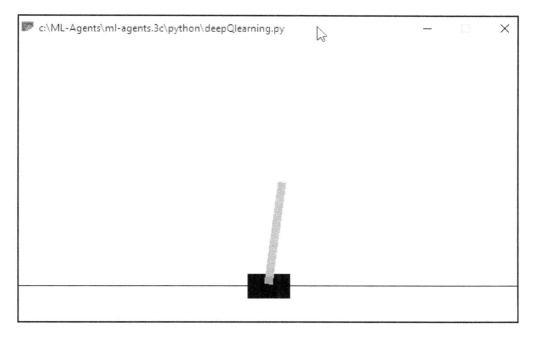

The gym environment running the cart-pole problem with Keras DQN

7. As the script runs, you will see the training output.

After the script runs, evaluate the results and determine if you need to increase the number of training runs or the network itself. Play around with the sample and see how you can improve on it.

Exploring the tensor

One of the things about Python that turns developers away is the loose typing. It can also be difficult to debug applications without the right tools, or with the right tools that are loosely typed. This gets more complicated when we start to look at complex mathematical types, such as tensors, in code. Fortunately, Visual Studio Code provides a simple Python debugger that can expose type inspection at runtime. Let's see how this works by going through the following exercise:

1. Open Visual Studio Code back up to the last exercise.
2. Set a breakpoint by clicking just in the margin of the editor, as shown in the following image:

```
20      model = Sequential()
21      model.add(Flatten(input_shape=(1,) + env.observa
22      model.add(Dense(16))
23      model.add(Activation('relu'))
24      model.add(Dense(nb_actions))
25      model.add(Activation('linear'))
26      print(model.summary())
27
28      policy = EpsGreedyQPolicy()
29      memory = SequentialMemory(limit=50000, window_le
30      dqn = DQNAgent(model=model, nb_actions=nb_action
31      target_model_update=1e-2, policy=policy)
32      dqn.compile(Adam(lr=1e-3), metrics=['mae'])
```

Setting a breakpoint in Visual Studio Code

3. From the menu, select **Debug | Start Debugging**. Let the code start and run. After the model is set up, the code will break at the set breakpoint.
4. Use your mouse to hover over the model text, as shown in the following screenshot:

```
 7
 8    from rl.    <keras.models.Sequential object at
 9    from rl.  ◢ input: <Tensor>
10    from rl.    ▷ OVERLOADABLE_OPERATORS: {'__truediv__', '_
11                ▷ _consumers: [<tf.Operation 'flatt...ype=Sh
12    ENV_NAME   ▷ _dtype: tf.float32
13                 _handle_data: None
14    # Get th     _id: 0                              ons available
15    env = gy   ▷ _keras_history: (<keras.engine.topolo...29
16    np.rando   ▷ _keras_shape: (None, 1, 4)
17    env.seed   ▷ _op: <tf.Operation 'flatten_1_input' type=
18    nb_actio   ◢ _shape: TensorShape([
19                 ▷ _dims: [Dimension(None), Dimension(1), Di
20    model =      ▷ dims: [Dimension(None), Dimension(1), Dim
21    model.ad       ndims: 3
22    model.ad     ▷ [0]: Dimension(None)              _space.shape))
23    model.ad     ▷ [1]: Dimension(1)
24    model.ad     ▷ [2]: Dimension(4)
25    model.ad      _uses_learning_phase: False
26    print(model.summary())   _value_index: 0
27
28    policy = EpsGreedyQPolicy()
```

Inspecting the neural network model and tensor types

5. After a second or so, the type **Inspector** window will pop up, allowing you to inspect the various properties.

6. Click the arrow beside `input:` `<Tensor>` to expand the input property.

7. Expand the `_shape` property as well.

8. You should see an input shape of three dimensions of 0, 1, and 4 dimensions respectively. This also happens to represent the shape of the input tensor. In this case, the input tensor is a flat, 1 x 4 array of inputs, which you can also think of as a single-row matrix or vector. We can represent a single value as a (0, 1, 1) shape, or any dimension of values with a tensor.

9. You can continue to explore the NN model and other variables on your own in this way.

Since the concept of a tensor as input can be quite confusing to newcomers, let's go over the concepts of tensors and tensor shapes. In the following diagram, we show a one-dimensional tensor that represents a single value all the way up to a six-dimensional tensor representing multiple values:

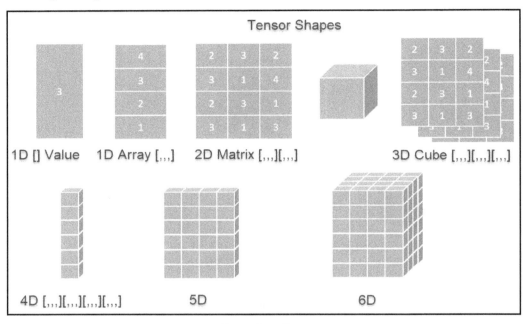

The many shapes of tensor

In our last example, the cart-pole problem, the tensor could be defined in multiple ways: as a 1D array; a 2D array/matrix of 1 x 4 or 4x1 values; as a 3D cube of (0, 1, 4) dimensions; and so on. The take-away from this is that we can represent any shape of data in the form of a tensor. You just have to make sure your data is in the correct shape; in fact, this will likely be your biggest issue when you go on to set up new networks on your own using Keras.

TensorFlow, our backend math engine, is of course named after the tensor. With most engines, you don't necessarily have to know how the internals work to use them, and TensorFlow is no exception. Therefore, we leave it up to the reader to further learn the internal workings of TensorFlow and Keras or other NN libraries on their own. Packt has numerous well-written books and videos on the subject.

There is a lot going on in this example, and hopefully you can appreciate the amount of work Keras is saving us. We chose this example because it featured the building of a model (network) without a lot of other plumbing. We won't explore any more of this example, but feel free to explore this code or other DQN agents more on your own. Fortunately for us, Unity has already taken care of mapping the observation of state and actions to the proper shapes. Going forward, we will use more of the advanced Unity Python code for building models, starting with proximal policy optimization in the next section.

Proximal policy optimization

Thus far, our discussion of RL has looked at simpler techniques for building agents with bandits and Q-learning. Q-learning is a popular algorithm, and as we learned, deep Q neural networks provide us with a great foundation to use to solve more difficult problems, such as a cart balancing a pole. The following table summarizes the various RL algorithms, what conditions they are capable of working in, and how they function:

Algorithm	Model	Policy	Action	Observation	Operator
Q-Learning	Model-free	Off-policy	Discrete	Discrete	Q value
SARSA – State Action Reward State Action	Model-free	On-policy	Discrete	Discrete	Q value
DQN – Deep Q Network	Model-free	Off-policy	Discrete	Continuous	Q value
DDPG – Deep Deterministic Policy Gradient	Model-free	Off-policy	Continuous	Continuous	Q value
TRPO – Trust Region Policy Optimization	Model-free	Off-policy	Continuous	Continuous	Advantage
PPO – Proximal Policy Optimization	Model-free	Off-policy	Continuous	Continuous	Advantage

As you can see from the preceding table, we went from the basics of Q-learning and accelerated to PPO, which is the preferred training method that Unity has developed. There are several terms in this table that we haven't explained, so let's cover them now in more detail so you can understand the differences between the various algorithms. The following is a short glossary of the terms provided in the table:

- **Model-free**: The algorithm does not depend on a defined model. Instead, the algorithm uses trial and error to map out its policy or course of action. All of the algorithms we will cover use model-free.

- **Off-policy**: Refers to how the brain/agent decides on its next course of action. If it is off-policy, the agent decides an action based on another policy, such as epsilon greedy or another method. We used epsilon greedy as our off-policy decision for the Q-learning examples.
- **On-policy**: Refers to the brain/agent making a decision based on the current policy, essentially the value of the action. SARSA is the only algorithm that uses an on-policy algorithm. A policy is what decides the agents actions.
- **Discrete**: Denotes how the space, be it action or observation, is divided into discrete steps or bins. We looked at discrete spaces in our Q-learning bandit examples.
- **Continuous**: The action or observation space can be continuous. In our DQN example, our action space was discrete, but the state or observation space was continuous. This gives us the advantage of feeding normalized continuous values into our model, as we saw in the cart-pole problem. In that example, the observed state was continuous, which provided us better fine-tuning. Discrete algorithms suffer from gaps in learning since they always need to be divided into a known set of values.
- **Q-value**: Raw Q values are used to make the decision, either when maximized or through some policy.
- **Advantage**: Q values are compared against other values for a range of actions determining which action provides the better advantage. This is no different than a game a of chess where you try to move your piece to a position of advantage based on your assessment of other moves.

A more formal introduction will cover the details of each algorithm in gross detail and at some length. Each algorithm of course shares its strengths and weaknesses but ultimately the best performer will be PPO for most of the problems we will tackle going forward. Therefore, let's take a look at PPO in action so we can see how it performs in the next section.

Implementing PPO

The implementation of PPO provided by Unity for training has been set up in a single script that we can put together quite quickly. Open up Unity to the unityenvironment sample projects and go through the following steps:

1. Locate the GridWorld scene in the Assets/ML-Agents/Examples/GridWorld folder. Double-click it to open it.

2. Locate the `GridWorldBrain` and set it to **External**.

3. If you have already set the project up to run minimized, then proceed to the next step. If not, you will need to go back to the *ML-Agents external brains* section to learn the required setup.

4. From the menu, select **File | Build Settings...**.

5. Uncheck any earlier scenes and be sure to click **Add Open Scenes** to add the `GridWorld` scene to the build.

6. Click **Build** to build the project, and again make sure that you put the output in the `python` folder. Again, if you are lost, refer to the *ML-Agents external brains* section.

7. Open a Python shell or Anaconda prompt window. Be sure to navigate to the `root` source folder, `ml-agents`.

8. Activate the `ml-agents` environment with the following:

```
activate ml-agents
```

9. From the `ml-agents` folder, run the following command:

```
python python/learn.py python/python.exe --run-id=grid1 --train
```

10. You may have to use Python 3 instead, depending on your Python engine. This will execute the `learn.py` script against the `python/python.exe` environment; be sure to put your executable name if you are not on Windows. Then we set a useful `run-id` we can use to identify runs later. Finally, we set the `--train` switch in order for the `agent/brain` to also be trained.

11. As the script runs, you should see the Unity environment get launched, and the shell window or prompt will start to show training statistics, as shown in the following screenshot of the console window:

```
Anaconda Prompt                                                    —   □   ×
INFO:unityagents: GridWorldBrain: Step: 464000. Mean Reward: 0.982. Std of Reward: 0.014.
INFO:unityagents: GridWorldBrain: Step: 466000. Mean Reward: 0.983. Std of Reward: 0.014.
INFO:unityagents: GridWorldBrain: Step: 468000. Mean Reward: 0.967. Std of Reward: 0.175.
INFO:unityagents: GridWorldBrain: Step: 470000. Mean Reward: 0.983. Std of Reward: 0.014.
INFO:unityagents: GridWorldBrain: Step: 472000. Mean Reward: 0.981. Std of Reward: 0.015.
INFO:unityagents: GridWorldBrain: Step: 474000. Mean Reward: 0.979. Std of Reward: 0.090.
INFO:unityagents: GridWorldBrain: Step: 476000. Mean Reward: 0.979. Std of Reward: 0.089.
INFO:unityagents: GridWorldBrain: Step: 478000. Mean Reward: 0.982. Std of Reward: 0.014.
INFO:unityagents: GridWorldBrain: Step: 480000. Mean Reward: 0.982. Std of Reward: 0.014.
INFO:unityagents: GridWorldBrain: Step: 482000. Mean Reward: 0.983. Std of Reward: 0.014.
INFO:unityagents: GridWorldBrain: Step: 484000. Mean Reward: 0.982. Std of Reward: 0.015.
INFO:unityagents: GridWorldBrain: Step: 486000. Mean Reward: 0.983. Std of Reward: 0.014.
INFO:unityagents: GridWorldBrain: Step: 488000. Mean Reward: 0.984. Std of Reward: 0.015.
INFO:unityagents: GridWorldBrain: Step: 490000. Mean Reward: 0.983. Std of Reward: 0.014.
INFO:unityagents: GridWorldBrain: Step: 492000. Mean Reward: 0.984. Std of Reward: 0.014.
INFO:unityagents: GridWorldBrain: Step: 494000. Mean Reward: 0.983. Std of Reward: 0.014.
INFO:unityagents: GridWorldBrain: Step: 496000. Mean Reward: 0.976. Std of Reward: 0.123.
INFO:unityagents: GridWorldBrain: Step: 498000. Mean Reward: 0.984. Std of Reward: 0.014.
INFO:unityagents:Saved Model
INFO:unityagents: GridWorldBrain: Step: 500000. Mean Reward: 0.979. Std of Reward: 0.089.
INFO:unityagents:Saved Model
INFO:unityagents:Saved Model
INFO:unityagents:List of nodes to export :
INFO:unityagents:          action
INFO:unityagents:          value_estimate
INFO:unityagents:          action_probs
INFO:tensorflow:Restoring parameters from ./models/grid1\model-500000.cptk
INFO:tensorflow:Restoring parameters from ./models/grid1\model-500000.cptk
INFO:tensorflow:Froze 8 variables.
INFO:tensorflow:Froze 8 variables.
```

Training output generated from learn.py

Let the training run for as long as it needs. Depending on your machine and the number of iterations, you could be looking at a few hours of training—yes, you read that right. As the environment is trained, you will see the agent moving around and getting reset over and over again. In the next section, we will take a closer look at what the statistics are telling us.

Understanding training statistics with TensorBoard

Inherently, ML has its roots in statistics, statistical analysis, and probability theory. While we won't strictly use statistical methods to train our models like some ML algorithms do, we will use statistics to evaluate training performance. Hopefully, you have some memory of high school statistics, but if not, a quick refresher will certainly be helpful.

The Unity PPO and other RL algorithms we will be using use a tool called TensorBoard, which allows us to evaluate statistics as an agent/environment is running. Go through the following steps as we run another Grid environment while watching the training with TensorBoard:

1. Open the `trainer_config.yaml` file in Visual Studio Code or another text editor. This file contains the various training parameters we use to train our models.

2. Locate the configuration for the `GridWorldBrain`, as shown in the following code:

```
GridWorldBrain:
    batch_size: 32
    normalize: false
    num_layers: 3
    hidden_units: 256
    beta: 5.0e-3
    gamma: 0.9
    buffer_size: 256
    max_steps: 5.0e5
    summary_freq: 2000
    time_horizon: 5
```

3. Change the `num_layers` parameter from 1 to 3, as shown in the highlighted code. This parameter sets the number of layers the neural network will have. Adding more layers allows our model to better generalize, which is a good thing. However, this will decrease our training performance, or the time it takes our agent to learn. Sometimes, this isn't a bad thing if you have the CPU/GPU to throw at training, but not all of us do, so evaluating training performance will be essential.

4. Open a command prompt or shell in the `ml-agents` folder and run the following command:

```
python python/learn.py python/python.exe --run-id=grid2 --train
```

5. Note how we updated the `--run-id` parameter to `grid2` from `grid1`. This will allow us to add another run of data and compare it to the last run in real time. This will run a new training session. If you have problems starting a session, make sure you are only running one environment at a time.

6. Open a new command prompt or shell window to the same `ml-agents` folder. Keep your other training window running.

7. Run the following command:

```
tensorboard --logdir=summaries
```

8. This will start the TensorBoard web server, which will serve up a web UI to view our training results.

9. Copy the hosting endpoint—typically `http://localhost:6006`, or perhaps the machine name—and paste it into a web browser. After a while, you should see the TensorBoard UI, as shown in the following screenshot:

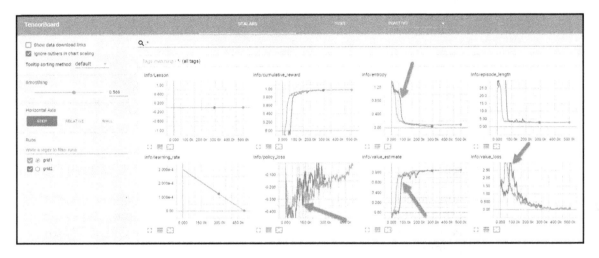

TensorBoard UI showing the results of training on GridWorld

You will need to wait a while to see progress from the second training session. When you do, though, as shown in the preceding image, you will notice that the new model (`grid2`) is lagging behind in training. Note how the blue line on each of the plots takes several thousand iterations to catch up. This is a result of the more general multilayer network. This isn't a big deal in this example, but on more complex problems, that lag could make a huge difference. While some of the plots show the potential for improvement—such as the entropy plot—overall, we don't see a significant improvement. Using a single-layer network for this example is probably sufficient.

We will explore these plots in detail in later chapters as we explore building more complex training/learning simulations. For now, take some time to run through the exercises in the next section.

Exercises

Complete the following exercises on your own:

1. Alter the `GridWorldBrain` parameters in the `trainer_config.yaml` file and run further training sessions to explore the effect of changing the parameters.
2. Build the `3DBalls` environment and train it with the `learn.py` PPO algorithm using an external brain.
3. Alter the parameters of the `trainer_config.yaml` file for the `Ball3DBrain`, run the simulation again, and view the results with TensorBoard.

Be sure to take some time to run through a few examples and configure some of the training parameters. Understanding what effect these hyperparameters can have on the impact of model training can be critical for you to successfully train working models.

Summary

In this chapter, we took a deep dive into the inner workings of more sophisticated RL algorithms, such as DQN and PPO. We started by walking through the installation of the Python tools and dependencies, where we learned how to use the more basic tools, such as Jupyter Notebook. Then we built a working ML-Agents example that used an external Python agent's brain. After that, we covered the basics of neurons and neural networks. From there, we took a look at DQN and a basic deep Q-learning agent using Keras. We completed the chapter by looking at another RL algorithm called PPO. As we learned, PPO will be the workhorse for many of our complex situations.

Our journey this chapter was more or less a setup for the next chapter, where we start to dig in deep and build on the foundations we laid in this chapter. We will take a closer look at PPO and how it can drive other more sophisticated learning scenarios in the next chapter.

4

Going Deeper with Deep Learning

At the end of the last chapter, we took a peek at what is possible with neural networks using an advanced RL algorithm called PPO. What we didn't cover are the details of how this code worked and what it is capable of. While teaching you about all the details of this model would take a book by itself, we will try and cover the basic features in this chapter. Also, keep in mind that while we will be talking about the Unity-specific training implementation, many of the concepts can be carried over to other deep learning models.

In this chapter, we will look at several concepts that are internal to the `learn.py` training script using PPO and by exploring the Unity ML-Agents examples. Here is what we will be covering in this chapter:

- Agent training problems
- Convolutional neural networks
- Experience replay
- Partial observability, memory, and recurrent networks
- Actor–critic training
- Exercises

 One thing to note is that our use of neural networks or deep learning solves a very specific problem. However, that doesn't mean that many of the same concepts you learn cannot be applied to other problems. Keep that in the back of your mind as you work through this chapter.

In this chapter, we are going to continue right from where we left off, so be sure you have completed the end of Chapter 3, *Deep Reinforcement Learning with Python* before continuing.

Agent training problems

Before we get into the more advanced techniques used inside Unity's training scripts, we want to understand a little more about how an agent's training can break. Let's open Unity back up to where we left off in the last chapter and see how easily we can break an agent's training using the following steps:

1. Open Unity to the **GridWorld** example exercise. If you need help with this, return to the last chapter and review the exercises.

2. Locate the **GridAcademy** object and component in the **Inspector** window and set the values as shown in the following excerpt:

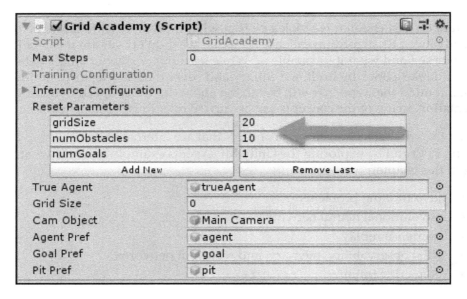

Setting the parameters for the grid example

3. Set the **gridSize** to 20, **numObstacles** to 10, and **numGoals** to 1, as shown in the preceding screenshot.

4. Set the **GridWorldBrain** to use a **Player** or **Heuristic** brain.

5. Press Play to run the sample, and look at the game. You should notice a much larger grid with plenty of extra obstacles. If you set the brain to **Player**, go ahead and play the game a couple times. Chances are you will run out of time, and so will our agent, which means we also need to increase the maximum step size.

Remember, we limit the agent's step size in order to avoid endless running agents. If we didn't do this, we could end up with agents that run for a very long time with little progress, or no progress at all if the agent's step size prevents them from completing the game. Conversely, too large a step size just slows down the training. So in order to reduce training times, we always try to minimize the agent's step size.

6. Press Play to stop the scene running.

7. Locate the **Grid Agent (Script)** object and component in the **Inspector** window, as shown in the following screenshot:

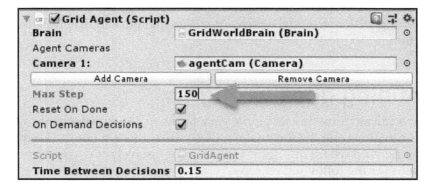

Setting the max step size on the grid agent

8. Set the **Max Step** size to 150, as shown in the preceding screenshot.

9. Set the **GridWorldBrain** back to use an **External** brain and build the **Unity** environment for external agent training, just as you did at the end of the last chapter, Chapter 3, *Deep Reinforcement Learning with Python*.

10. Again, referring back to the last chapter if necessary, run the `learn.py` training script. You may want to change the `run-id` parameter to `grid3` or something later in order to visualize the results in TensorBoard.

11. Let the agent run for about `16 000` to `20 000` iterations, as shown in the following screenshot:

```
INFO:unityagents: GridWorldBrain: Step: 2000. Mean Reward: -1.394. Std of Reward: 0.468.
INFO:unityagents: GridWorldBrain: Step: 4000. Mean Reward: -1.390. Std of Reward: 0.733.
INFO:unityagents: GridWorldBrain: Step: 6000. Mean Reward: -1.319. Std of Reward: 0.490.
INFO:unityagents: GridWorldBrain: Step: 8000. Mean Reward: -1.273. Std of Reward: 0.683.
INFO:unityagents: GridWorldBrain: Step: 10000. Mean Reward: -1.158. Std of Reward: 0.647.
INFO:unityagents: GridWorldBrain: Step: 12000. Mean Reward: -1.413. Std of Reward: 0.274.
INFO:unityagents: GridWorldBrain: Step: 14000. Mean Reward: -1.109. Std of Reward: 0.883.
INFO:unityagents: GridWorldBrain: Step: 16000. Mean Reward: -1.251. Std of Reward: 0.472.
INFO:unityagents: GridWorldBrain: Step: 18000. Mean Reward: -1.203. Std of Reward: 0.593.
INFO:unityagents: GridWorldBrain: Step: 20000. Mean Reward: -1.199. Std of Reward: 0.672.
```

Agent results from training

What we are seeing here is inconsistent training convergence, which is a sign that something is wrong with our model or scenario. We will take a look at how to fix this issue in the next section.

When training goes wrong

It should come as no surprise that it is quite easy for us to get ourselves into situations where training can go wrong. Unfortunately, these situations are not the kind with big explosions, but the kind where our agent will not progressively learn or improve. This typically happens for the following reasons:

- **Reward is wrong (sparse rewards)**: Generally, you want to stay within a range of `-1.0` to `+1.0` and have readily available rewards.
- **Observations are wrong**: Too many or too few observations can be a problem, depending on the model.
- **Hyper parameters**: This encompasses many parameters, and not understanding how to adjust these can lead to frustration. We will, of course, spend some time learning how to properly adjust these parameters.

We will cover the first two in more detail over the next couple sections. We will cover the third at some length over the course of the remaining chapter.

Fixing sparse rewards

Reward issues can happen when you attempt to set the rewards too high or low, or when the opportunity for a reward is rare or sparse. In our last example, when we expanded the grid to an area of 20 x 20 from an area of 5 x 5, we also made our reward very sparse or rare. That means that an agent needs to be especially lucky in order to stumble upon a reward. We can improve this by increasing the number of goals available. Go through the following steps to correct the problem of sparse rewards:

1. Open up the Unity editor and locate the Grid Academy object and component in the **Inspector** window.
2. Set the **numGoals** property to 10. Increasing the number of goals should allow the agent to more easily stumble upon a positive reward.
3. Build the environment and run a training session with learn.py. You should see the agents' training quickly converge.

Reward issues are generally easy to fix and should be the first thing you tackle if your agent is slow to train. In the next section, we will look at how we resolve issues with the incorrect observation space.

Fixing the observation of state

Making sure you are capturing the relevant observation of state for your agent is critical to successfully train an agent. In most of the earlier examples, the way in which we built the observation of state was quite simplistic, but as you can now appreciate, an agent's state can be quite substantial. In fact, some RL problems currently being tackled have states exceeding the number of atoms in the known universe—yes, you read that right. We broached this subject in the last chapter, where we demonstrated how the agent observations could be mapped as inputs onto a neural network. When setting up the Unity external brain trainer, it will be essential that you understand the how or what of things that an agent needs to observe.

In order to fix our current issue, or make our agent better at training, we will expand our agent's state. In expanding our agent's state, our agent should be able to interrupt more details. After all, our agent is using a visual observation of the play area as its sense of state. The following exercise shows how we can improve training by expanding the agent's state or visual observation:

1. Locate the **GridWorldBrain** and adjust the **Visual Observation** space, as shown in the following screenshot:

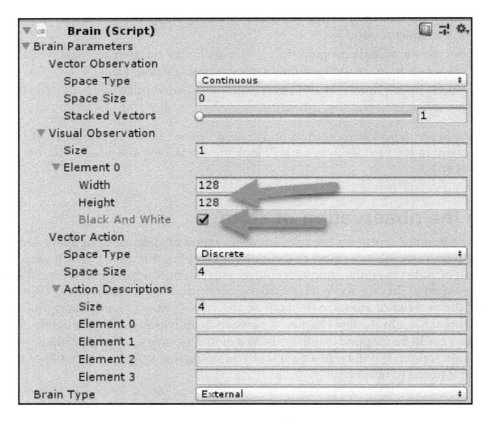

Adjusting the visual observation space for the agent

2. The **GridWorldBrain** uses **Visual Observation** as a view of state. Essentially, the agent is using a separate camera to take screenshots of the game area and interprets these as the state.

3. Select the **agentcam** in the scene. This will show you the view the agent sees. The agent uses this camera to take snapshots of the scene at every step and transfer them as raw images to the brain. The previous settings of an 84 x 84 area using color weren't large enough to capture the details of the increase in grid size. Therefore, we need to increase the resolution, but because our objects are denoted by shape, we can probably drop color as well. The following is an example of the 84 x 84 color image against the 128 x 128 black-and-white image:

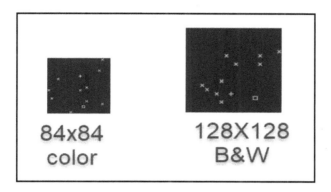

Comparison of visual observation spaces

4. The agent consumes each pixel and color channel in the image as a normalized input in the internal neural network. A normalized input is encoded to a range of 0–1.0.

5. Make sure the **brain** is set to **External** and build the project.

6. Run the environment again with the **PPO** model using learn.py. Depending on your Python environment of choice, you may have to use python3 to start instead of python:

```
python python/learn.py python/python.exe --run-id=largegrid1 --train
```

7. Watch the agent run again. You will notice a slight improvement, but not much.

8. Increase the **GridWorldBrain Visual Observation** space to 256 x 256 from the previous 128 x 128 and make sure that you uncheck **Black and White**.

9. Build and run the environment again. You should see much better training results now, as your agent will show some signs of convergence. Keep playing with the model and see how you can improve it further.

By playing with the color and increasing the observation space from 84 x 84 to 256 x 256, we were able to play with a much larger visual state in order to create a working/learning agent, albeit considerably slower. See if you can guesstimate the optimal **Visual Observation** dimensions between a value of 84 -> 256. After you test the dimensions, see what effect enabling/disabling the use of color does to the learning process.

 If you find you are still having trouble training, increase the numGoals parameter again. In the original example, we had a reward for every 25 cells in a 5 x 5 grid. When we upped our grid dimensions to 20 x 20 with 10 goals the ratio of area to rewards was still at 40 grid cells to 1 reward (400/10 = 40).

The research done with the classic 80's Atari games that used RL to teach an agent to play better than a human used the same method to capture state. However, we can't just interpret the state from an image without a little preprocessing. Fortunately, the Unity trainers have already incorporated this feature in the form of convolution neural networks, which we will cover in the next section.

Convolutional neural networks

A lot of work has been done over the years in using neural networks to perform image recognition, and along the way, a technique called the convolutional neural network was developed to provide a better method of identifying features in images. This technique works by running a convolution step across the image, as shown in the following diagram:

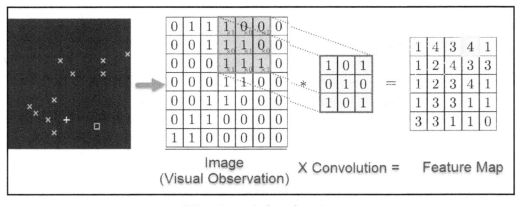

CNN operation extracting features from an image

What is happening here is that a convolution matrix set by stride is multiplied across the image using a convolution step in order to generate a feature map. We do this in order to isolate features in an image by isolating sections of pixels and applying a grouping filter. If we didn't do this, our network would evaluate the image's raw pixels, which would make recognizing important features in an image difficult. It's not unlike looking at a picture that is far too close. In applications where an NN is used to recognize images, we often use a corresponding pooling layer and then another convolution layer followed by another pooling layer. However, this can simplify an image so much that it removes spatial information from the data. Consequently, in games and simulations that require spatial awareness, we discard the pooling layers and instead just use convolutional layers. Go through the following exercise to see how the learn.py trainer uses CNN layers:

1. Revert the **GridWorld** sample back to using a 5 x 5 grid, as well as one goal and one obstacle. Build the environment as you have done plenty of times before.
2. Open a shell or explorer window and navigate to the python folder inside the ml-agents folders.
3. Locate and open the models.py file in the unitytrainers folder in Visual Studio Code or your favorite Python editor.
4. Scroll down until you find the create_visual_encoder function:

```
def create_visual_encoder(self, image_input, h_size, activation,
num_layers):
    """
    Builds a set of visual (CNN) encoders.
    :param image_input: The placeholder for the image input to use.
    :param h_size: Hidden layer size.
    :param activation: What type of activation function to
    use for layers.
    :param num_layers: number of hidden layers to create.
    :return: List of hidden layer tensors.
    """
        conv1 = tf.layers.conv2d(image_input, 16, kernel_size=[8, 8],
        strides=[4, 4], activation=tf.nn.elu)
        conv2 = tf.layers.conv2d(conv1, 32, kernel_size=[4, 4],
        strides=[2, 2], activation=tf.nn.elu)
        hidden = c_layers.flatten(conv2)
        for j in range(num_layers):
            hidden = tf.layers.dense(hidden, h_size, use_bias=False,
            activation=activation)
        return hidden
```

5. This function creates two convolution layers, first with a 8 x 8 kernel and then with a 4 x 4 kernel, followed by a `flatten` operation that flattens into a hidden layer for every layer in the `num_layers` parameter. This is a fairly standard configuration, but we can also play with this to see what effect it has on the training. We are going to add another layer of convolution in order to hopefully identify more features.

6. Modify the code in the `create_visual_encoder` method, as shown in the following code:

```
conv1 = tf.layers.conv2d(image_input, 16, kernel_size=[8,8],
strides=[4, 4],
activation=tf.nn.elu) conv2 = tf.layers.conv2d(conv1, 32,
kernel_size=[4, 4], strides=[2, 2], activation=tf.nn.elu) conv3 =
tf.layers.conv2d(conv2, 64, kernel_size=[2, 2], strides=[1, 1],
activation=tf.nn.elu) hidden = c_layers.flatten(conv3)
```

7. What we did here is just chain in another convolutional layer, doubling the number of inputs and reducing the size by half, just as we did in the previous layer. Ideally, this may allow us to extract more features to aid us in training. Now, we have three convolution layers progressively pulling feature maps, one after the other.

8. Save the changes in the file.

9. Run `learn.py` with the following command:

```
python python/learn.py python/python.exe --run-id=gridconv1 --train
```

10. Hopefully, by the end of this chapter, you will be able to run `learn.py` in your sleep. Watch the training and try to get a feel for how this new layer improved the training performance. Did it? Looks like you will have to try the sample in order to find out.

That covers the basics of CNN layers for now. Most of the other Unity samples we run won't use visual observations to capture the state. However, we will revisit CNNs in the last chapter, `Chapter 6`, *Terrarium Revisited – A Multi-Agent Ecosystem*. Until then, there is plenty more information online about how to set the kernel size and stride so interested readers can just Google CNN.

In the next section, we will take a close look at what experience replay is and how the Unity trainers use it for training.

Experience replay

Since our first example of DQN, we have been using experience replay internally to more efficiently train an agent. ER involves nothing more than storing the agent's experiences in the form of a `<state, action, reward, next state>` tuple that fills a buffer. The agent then randomly walks or samples through this buffer of experiences in training. This has the benefit of keeping the agent more generalized and avoiding localized patterns. The following is an updated diagram of what our learning flow looks like when we add experience replay:

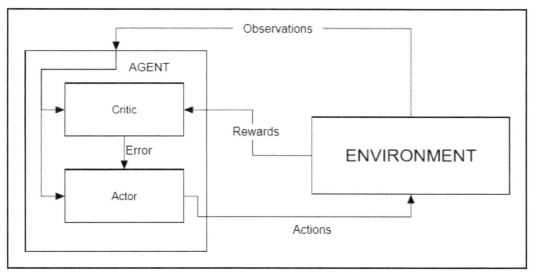

Diagram of RL with experience replay added

In the preceding diagram, you can see how the agent stores experiences in a buffer memory that it then randomly samples from at each step. As the buffer fills, older experiences are discarded. This may seem quite counter-intuitive, since our goal is to find the best or optimal path, so lets explore this concept further with the following exercise:

1. Open up Unity to the ML-Agents sample projects and open the **Hallway** sample scene in the `Assets/ML-Agents/Examples/Hallway/Scenes` folder.

2. Locate and set the **HallwayBrain Brain Type** to **External** in the **Inspector** window.

3. From the menu, select **File** | **Build Settings....**
4. Be sure to uncheck or remove all the scenes, except for the **Hallway** scene. You can use the **Add Open Scenes** button to add the current scene if it is not already on the list.
5. Build the scene as you would for **External** training.
6. Open up your `Python` shell or Anaconda prompt.
7. Activate the **ml-agents** environment with **Activate Ml-Agents**.
8. Navigate to the `ml-agents` source folder and execute the following command:

```
python python/learn.py python/python.exe --run-id=hallway1 --train
```

This will run the default training that Unity configured with the sample. Remember, we can access the training parameters in the `trainer_config.yaml` file, found in the `python` folder.

As you run the default example, notice how poorly the agent functions. The reason for this is that the agent's current experience buffer is too small. If you select the Unity environment window, you will see that the agent tends to stay at one end of the hallway and is rarely able to find an optimum path to the goal (reward). We can alleviate this issue by increasing the size of the experience buffer and, in essence, the agent's short-term memory.

Building on experience

While an agent trains, the experience buffer recycles old memories and replaces them with new ones. As we discussed, the purpose of this is to break any localized patterns or, essentially, situations where the agent just repeats itself. The downside of this, however, is that the agent may forget what the endgame is, which is what happened in the last example. We can simply fix this by increasing the size of the experience buffer, which we will do in the next exercise:

1. Open Visual Studio Code or your favorite text editor.
2. Locate the `trainer_config.yaml` file in the `python` folder and open it.
3. Locate the configuration for the `HallwayBrain`, as shown in the following code:

```
HallwayBrain:
  use_recurrent: true
  sequence_length: 64
  num_layers: 2
  hidden_units: 128
  memory_size: 256
  beta: 1.0e-2
```

```
gamma: 0.99
num_epoch: 3
buffer_size: 1024
batch_size: 128
max_steps: 5.0e5
summary_freq: 1000
time_horizon: 64
```

4. The `buffer_size` parameter represents the size of the experience buffer. We want to increase this so that our agent can sample from a larger buffer or from a larger state or set of experiences. This is very similar to the issue we saw earlier when our agent was not able to explore the entire play area. In that case, we increased the number of steps the agent could take in an episode or training session.

5. Increase the `buffer_size` to `4096`, essentially quadrupling it, as shown in the following code:

```
buffer_size: 4096
```

6. Save the file and run the trainer again, but change `--run-id` to `hallway2`, as shown in the following code:

```
python python/learn.py python/python.exe --run-id=hallway2 --train
```

7. This will run the agent and, after a few hours, open TensorBoard with the following command in a new command prompt:

```
tensorboard --logdir=summaries
```

8. Compare the results of the different experience buffer sizes, as shown in the following code:

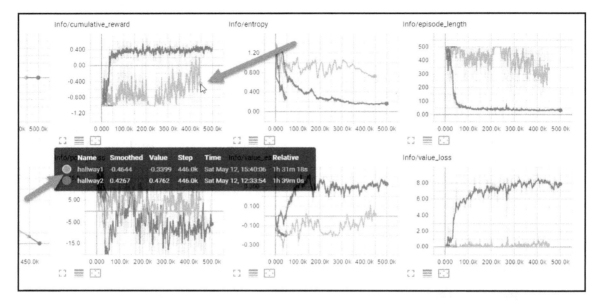

Comparison of training runs using different experience buffer sizes

9. Hover your mouse over the graphs to see a training comparison, as shown in the preceding screenshot. As you can see, the difference in training is remarkable. By increasing the buffer size, the agent was quickly able to reach a good cumulative reward. However, the agent is quickly reaching a maximum of around `0.5-ish` (`0.4267 hallway2`), which means that the performance is good but not great. In fact, we may have overcorrected.

Comparing training examples—as we just did by just tweaking a single parameter—is a great way to learn more about the effect they will have on each model or parameter. One process of training is to select the minimum/maximum parameter values of a parameter and train for each extreme to see the effect. In our last exercise, we likely would have chosen a maximum value for the experience buffer, but if we were not sure, we could have run another training session with a higher value. After we find the minimum/maximum range, then we can try and optimize a parameter within that range.

If you use the minimum/maximum method of training, just remember that you should only change one parameter at a time. You may also find an optimum parameter that isn't so optimum when another parameter changes. This can be challenging when you first start out, so do your best to be patient and train, train, train.

As we have seen, using an experience buffer has its limitations, and ideally we want a better method to represent an agent's longer term memory. There is a little more going on with the `Hallway` example than we first saw, and we will discuss that big change in the next section.

Partial observability, memory, and recurrent networks

One major difference between the `Hallway` and `GridWorld` examples is their perception of state, or observation. We already know that the `GridWorld` agent used visual observations, but we never really got into what state input the `Hallway` agent used. As it turns out, the `Hallway` agent collects observations of state in a different manner. It is important for us to understand the difference, so open up Unity and go through the following exercise:

1. Make sure the `Hallway` example scene is loaded. Check back to the previous exercise if you need help.
2. Locate the `Agent` object in the **Hierarchy** window. You can use the search bar at the top of the window to find it quicker.
3. Find the `Hallway Agent` component/script in the **Inspector** window.
4. Click the target icon beside the component and select **Edit Script....** This will open your previously set code editor.
5. Locate the `CollectObservation` method in the script shown in the following code:

```
public override void CollectObservations()
{
  float rayDistance = 12f;
  float[] rayAngles = { 20f, 60f, 90f, 120f, 160f };
  string[] detectableObjects = { "orangeGoal", "redGoal",
  "orangeBlock",
   "redBlock", "wall" };
  AddVectorObs((float)GetStepCount() /
(float)agentParameters.maxStep);
  AddVectorObs(rayPer.Perceive(rayDistance, rayAngles,
```

```
        detectableObjects, 0f,
        0f));
}
```

6. Some of this code is hopefully a little familiar, as we already wrote our own versions of `CollectObservations` previously. Remember that the calls to `AddVectorObs` are what add state to our agent's brain. The first call sets a single float, representing the agent's progress that's the calculation that is being done. The next call to `AddVectorObs` is where the action happens, and needs a closer look.

7. Hover your mouse over the `rayPer.Percieve` text and note the comment **Creates perception vector to be used as part of an observation of an agent**. This call is what builds the observation of state based on the projection of rays from the agent. The following is a simple visual showing you what is happening:

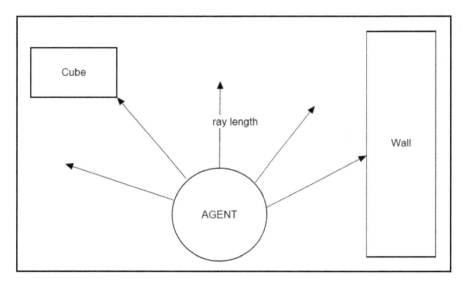

Agent using raycasting to observe state

8. What is happening here is that Unity is using its physics raycasting system to detect specific objects. It casts a ray for each type of object it wants to detect, and at every angle. When an object is detected, we also want to provide information for how far away it is. We also want to know when an object is not detected. If you look at the code for `rayPer.Percieve` you will see that it creates an array that is the size of the `angles X (the number of object types +2)`. The extra `+2` is to account for encoding distance and misses. In our example, this creates an array of `5 (angles) x (5 object types +2) = 35 cells`. When we add the previous call to `AddVectorObs`, we can see our agent uses a state of 36 floats.

You can go back to Unity and confirm that the **Vector Observation** size on the **HallwayBrain** is set to using continuous with a size of `36`. If you wanted to add object types to this example, you would need to recalculate this parameter. Of course, there is still more going on here. Have you figured it out yet? Perhaps the next section will help.

Partial observability

One of the first things to note that may not be so obvious is that our agent is no longer reliant on the full knowledge of its environment, as it was in all our other examples. In **GridWorld**, for instance, the agent viewed the entire play area with a camera and used the acquired images as its observation of state. But is it therefore realistic for us to assume that an agent needs to understand the whole play area of a world? Not likely, and this certainly doesn't happen in our go-to reference, nature. In nature, animals certainly don't know everything about the world—far from it. An animal only interacts with a partial view of its environment, dictated by its senses of sight, sound, touch, and so on. This allows an animal to better generalize its behavior to situations and environments. This certainly sounds like something our agents need to do.

Fortunately, the PPO trainer provides powerful support for problems of partial observability when an agent can only see a partial view of their world. However, in order to understand this better, let's revisit the `Hallway` example and turn off a feature that is allowing our agent to learn using only a partial view of the world. Open up Visual Studio Code and go through the following steps:

1. Open up `trainer_config.yaml` and edit the highlighted values shown in the following screenshot:

```
HallwayBrain:
    use_recurrent: false
    sequence_length: 64
```

```
num_layers: 2
hidden_units: 128
memory_size: 256
beta: 1.0e-2
gamma: 0.99
num_epoch: 3
buffer_size: 4096
batch_size: 128
max_steps: 5.0e5
summary_freq: 1000
time_horizon: 64
```

2. If you want, use a more optimum `buffer_size` value that you tested from the previous experience buffer exercise.

3. Open up your Python environment to the `python` folder with the **ml-agents** environment activated.

4. Launch the trainer with the following:

```
python python/learn.py python/python.exe --run-id=hallway3 --train
```

5. Watch the console training output carefully. You will likely see brief periods where the agent learns well, but then seems to forget everything. Some of this has to do with the experience buffer, but the rest occurs because our agent is forgetting what it has learned.

 We have converted our problem from a Markov decision process to partially observed Markov decision process, or POMDP for short.

Let the entire training session run for comparison, and be sure to monitor the results with TensorBoard. By turning off the `use_recurrent` option, we essentially disabled the agents' use of recurrent network layers. These recurrent layers act as another form of extended memory that we will cover in the next section.

Memory and recurrent networks

By taking away an agent's omniscient powers of full observation, we need to allow our agent to better generalize, and thus be able to learn long term. We do this by adding recurrent layers or blocks that are composed of long-short-term-memory cells, or LSTM layers.

These layers/cells provide the temporal memory for our agent and work as shown in the following diagram:

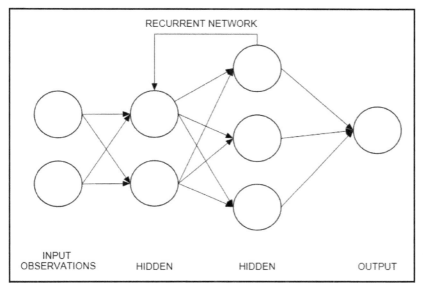

Recurrent networks

A recurrent network is essentially a bridge between a couple of hidden layers in the network that reinforce good or bad experiences back through the network. We can look at how this works in code by going through the following exercise:

1. Open Visual Studio Code.
2. Locate the models.py file in the **python/unitytrainers** folder. Be sure that the class in the file is LearningModel and not PPOModel.
3. Scroll down to the create_recurrent_encoder method, as shown in the following code:

```
def create_recurrent_encoder(self, input_state, memory_in,
name='lstm'):
    """
    Builds a recurrent encoder for either state or observations
    (LSTM).
    :param input_state: The input tensor to the LSTM cell.
    :param memory_in: The input memory to the LSTM cell.
    :param name: The scope of the LSTM cell.
    """
    s_size = input_state.get_shape().as_list()[1]
    m_size = memory_in.get_shape().as_list()[1]
```

```
lstm_input_state = tf.reshape(input_state, shape=[-1,
self.sequence_length,
s_size])
_half_point = int(m_size / 2)
with tf.variable_scope(name):
    rnn_cell = tf.contrib.rnn.BasicLSTMCell(_half_point)
    lstm_vector_in = tf.contrib.rnn.LSTMStateTuple(memory_in[:,
    :_half_point], memory_in[:, _half_point:])
    recurrent_state, lstm_state_out = tf.nn.dynamic_rnn(rnn_cell,
    lstm_input_state,
    initial_state=lstm_vector_in, time_major=False,
    dtype=tf.float32)
    recurrent_state = tf.reshape(recurrent_state,
    shape=[-1, _half_point])
    return recurrent_state, tf.concat([lstm_state_out.c,
    lstm_state_out.h],
    axis=1)
```

4. Now, this code is a little beyond the level we want to explore in this book, but hopefully just looking at the code can give you some insight into how it works. What we can see here is that the code is using LSTM cells to store memory that it then feeds back to the network. Unlike the experience buffer memory that is randomly sampled, we keep an ordered state of events. You may often hear this referred to as temporal memory. Temporal memory allows our agents to be more spatially aware, and this is a very good thing for most games and simulations.

5. Open up the `trainer_config.yaml` file, yet again, and modify the parameters as shown in the following code:

```
HallwayBrain:
    use_recurrent: true
    sequence_length: 128
    num_layers: 2
    hidden_units: 128
    memory_size: 1024
    beta: 1.0e-2
    gamma: 0.99
    num_epoch: 3
    buffer_size: 4096
    batch_size: 128
    max_steps: 5.0e5
    summary_freq: 1000
    time_horizon: 128
```

6. In this section of configuration, we are turning back on the recurrent networks and increasing the memory size. Remember that our previous agent training sessions were still falling short of a full 1.0 reward. Therefore, we will take this opportunity to increase the temporal memory of the agent. We set `use_recurrent` to true, `sequence_length` to 128, `memory_size` to 1024, `buffer_size` to 4096, and `time_horizon` to 128. This sets a recurrent network with a memory size of 1024 and a sequence length of 128. The sequence length sets the number of steps the agent remembers. We follow that by updating the experience buffer size to 4096 and the number of sampled steps to 128.

7. Open up Unity to the **Hallway** example scene. You should be able to do this in your sleep by now.

8. Locate the HallwayBrain object in the **Hierarchy** and **Inspector** windows.

9. Set the **Vector Observations Stacked Vectors** slider as shown in the following screenshot:

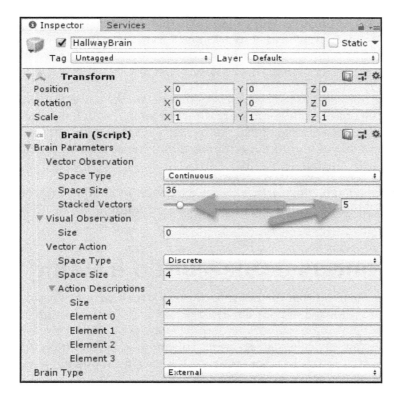

Setting the vector observation stack size

10. This sets the number of temporal steps we want our agent to remember. We also need to adjust the `memory_size` parameter to account for this. We already did this previously.

11. Build the training environment and place the output in the `python` folder.

12. Open a Python or Anaconda prompt, if one is not already open. Navigate to the `ml-agents` folder and activate `ml-agents`.

13. Run the trainer with the following:

```
python python/learn.py python/python.exe --run-id=hallway4 --train
```

14. Watch the console output closely. You may initially notice that the agent just seems to wander, and does no better than our initial runs. However, at some point, the agent will hit the reward a few times, and then it quickly learns the pattern using memory. Then, the agent will quickly surpass our previous training efforts by around 50,000 iterations, possibly sooner.

Feel free to go back and optimize this example further. If you are interested in more information about recurrent neural networks and LSTM cells, there is always plenty online. Keep in mind that this is an advanced topic and will require you understand more internal details about neural networks than this book has covered.

By understanding how best to use recurrent neural networks in the last example, we saw the power of partial observability and providing our agents with temporal memory. After you train the last example, you may still notice that the agent is still struggling. See if you can increase the number of temporal vector states and the amount of memory to optimize the agent further.

In the next section, we will look further under the covers at another major improvement PPO uses over DQN—a technique called actor–critic training.

Asynchronous actor – critic training

Thus far, we have assumed that the internal training structure of PPO mirrors what we learned when we first looked at neural networks and DQN. However, this isn't actually the case. Instead of using a single network to derive *Q* values or some form of policy, the PPO algorithm uses a technique called actor–critic. This method is essentially a combination of calculating values and policy. In actor–critic, or A3C, we train two networks. One network acts as a *Q*-value estimate or critic, and the other determines the policy or actions of the actor or agent.

We compare these values in the following equation to determine the advantage:

$$Advantage : A = Q(s, a) - V(s)$$

However, the network is no longer calculating Q-values, so we substitute that for an estimation of rewards:

$$Advantage : A = R - V(s)$$

Now our environment looks like the following screenshot:

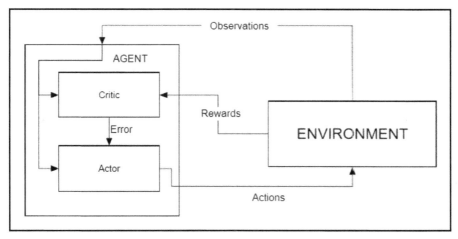

Diagram of actor–critic network

The error term that is communicated between the critic and actor is derived from the following equations:

$$ValueLoss : L = \Sigma(R - V(s))^2 (SumSquaredError)$$

$$PolicyLoss : L = -log(\pi(a|s)) * A(s)$$

Our intention here is to minimize the error, but a better term/equation to use is the calculation of entropy:

$$H(\pi) = -\Sigma(P(x)log(P(x)))$$

Entropy ($H(\pi)$) measures the spread of probability, while a high entropy represents an agent with multiple similar actions, which makes the agent's decisions difficult. A smaller value for entropy equates to an agent that can make better-informed decisions. This updates our loss function to the following:

$$PolicyLoss : L = -log(\pi(a|s)) * A(s) - \beta * H(\pi)$$

Finally, when we combine the two loss functions, value and policy, we get the final equation for loss, as shown in the following:

$$L = 0.5 * \Sigma(R - V(s))^2 - log(\pi(a|s)) * A(s) - \beta * H(\pi)$$

This loss function is the one our network (agent) is trying to minimize. While this is the form of training we have been using since the beginning to use PPO, we have omitted one other critical improvement. Actor–critic training was derived to work with multiple asynchronous agents, each working within their own environment. We will explore the asynchronous side of training in the next section.

Multiple asynchronous agent training

The A3C algorithm we just looked at was developed by Google DeepMind as a way of training multiple asynchronous agents simultaneously into a global overseer network. Now the Hallway example is already set up for multiple asynchronous training, and we can turn it on relatively quickly. Open up Unity and go through the following exercise to enable multiple agent training:

1. Open the **Hallway** example scene.

2. Locate and select the **Hallway(1)** to **Hallway(15)** objects, as shown in the following screenshot:

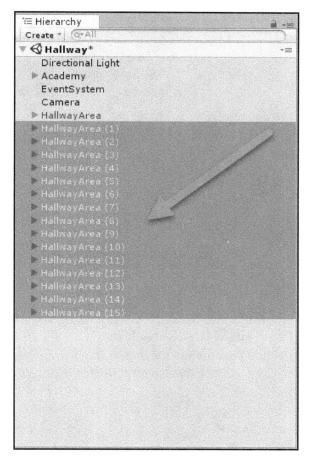

Selecting the disabled Hallway objects

3. Enable all these objects by checking the **Enable** box in the **Inspector** window. You should see all the objects turn from faded to solid when they become active. We just enabled another 15 training environments, all set around the **Hallway** environment.

4. Zoom your camera out and you will see 16 **Hallway** environments, as shown in the following screenshot:

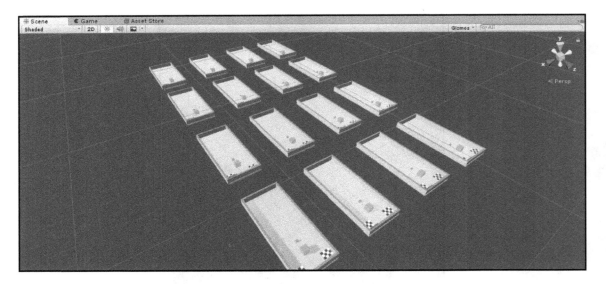

Turning on all the Hallway environments and agents

5. Open the build settings and build the environment. We will still build a single Unity player to run all the environments in.

6. Set the configuration parameters for the `HallwayBrain` in the `trainer_config.yaml` file, as shown in the following code:

```
HallwayBrain:
  use_recurrent: true
  sequence_length: 256
  num_layers: 2
  hidden_units: 128
  memory_size: 4096
  beta: 1.0e-2
  gamma: 0.99
  num_epoch: 3
  buffer_size: 4096
  batch_size: 128
  max_steps: 5.0e5
  summary_freq: 500
  time_horizon: 64
```

7. Open a `Python` or Anaconda prompt. Activate the `ml-agents` and navigate to the `ml-agents` folder.

8. Run the trainer with the following:

```
python python/learn.py python/python.exe --run-id=hallwayA3C --train
```

9. While the trainer is running, you will only see 1 environment, which is alright, but in reality, 16 environments and agents are running.

Adding the additional memory and agents will make the training much slower, although you may not notice much of a difference at first. The reason for this is that the agent's memory needs to resolve a number of consistent good memories. Once the agent is able to do this consistently, you will notice an improvement in training. Take a look at the following TensorBoard output and note the convergence of entropy:

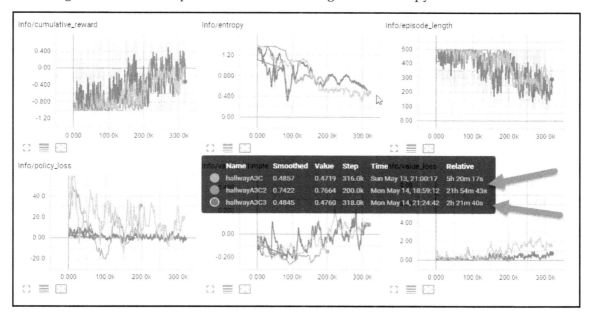

Convergence of entropy showing the agent making better decisions more quickly

The main thing to note in this graph that is a clear indication that training is going well is the entropy graph. Remember how we minimized the entropy in our equations, and that a smaller value meant that the agent was making better decisions? A better, more elegant configuration for the `Hallway` example is shown in the following code:

```
HallwayBrain:
  use_recurrent: true
  sequence_length: 32
  num_layers: 1
  hidden_units: 128
  memory_size: 512
  beta: 1.0e-2
  gamma: 0.99
  num_epoch: 3
  buffer_size: 1024
  batch_size: 128
  max_steps: 5.0e5
  summary_freq: 500
  time_horizon: 64
```

The preceding configuration is much leaner than what we had previously been running. We reduced the number of layers, the amount of memory, sequence, buffer, and time horizon parameters. As always, feel free to go back and play with the last example, further exploring the parameters in other training sessions. Alternatively, you can review and perform the exercises in the next section for more experience.

Exercises

Use the following exercises to improve your understanding of RL and the PPO trainer.

1. Convert one of the Unity examples to use just visual observations. Hint, use the **GridWorld** example as a guide, and remember that the agent may need its own camera.

2. Alter the CNN configuration of an agent using visual observations in three different ways. You can add more layers, take them away, or alter the kernel filter. Run the training sessions and compare the differences with TensorBoard.

3. Convert the **GridWorld** sample to use vector observations and recurrent networks with memory. Hint, you can borrow several pieces of code from the `Hallway` example.

4. Revisit the `Ball3D` example and set it up to use multiple asynchronous agent training.
5. Set up the crawler example and run it with multiple asynchronous agent training.

If you encounter problems running through these samples, be sure to check online. These samples will likely be well worn, with many other people tweaking or enhancing them further.

Summary

In this chapter, we took a closer look at the Unity PPO trainer. This training model, originally developed at OpenAI, is the current advanced model, and was our focus for starting to build more complex training scenarios. We first revisited the `GridWorld` example to understand what happens when training goes wrong. From there, we looked at some examples of situations where training is performing sub par, and we learned how to fix some of those issues. Then, we learned how an agent can use visual observations as input into our model, providing the data is processed first. We learned that an agent using visual observation required the use of CNN layers to process and extract features from images. After that, we looked at the value of using experience replay in order to further generalize our models. This taught us that experience and memory were valuable to an agent's training, so much so that we looked at a more advanced form of memory called recurrent neural networks. With recurrent blocks of LSTM cells, our agent also no longer needed to observe the entire game area. Instead, our agents could now use a technique called partial observability in order to manage state and awareness. Finally, we finished off the chapter by looking at an advanced technique called asynchronous actor–critic, or A3C, training. This form of training uses an internal critic and actor to manage the minimization of errors across multiple asynchronous agents.

In the next chapter, we will introduce further training techniques using multiple agents in various configurations, where we will have agents play against each other or work with each other to solve learning problems.

Playing the Game

5

We have already covered some very sophisticated examples and built some fairly intelligent agents. The techniques we have learned to use with RL and more specifically, PPO, are cutting edge, but as we learned, they still have their limitations. ML researchers continue to push the limits in multiple areas like network architecture and training setup. In the last chapter, we looked at one style of training multiple agents in multiple environments. In this chapter, we will explore the various novel training strategies we can employ with multiple agents and/or brains in an environment, from adversarial and cooperative self-play to imitation and curriculum learning. This will cover most of the remaining Unity examples, and the following is a summary of the main topics we will cover:

- Multi-agent environments
- Adversarial self-play
- Decisions and on-demand decision making
- Imitation learning
- Curriculum learning
- Exercises

We will continue right where we left off from the last chapter, more or less, meaning you should be very comfortable setting up and running a trainer now. If you have not run training sessions with an external brain yet, be sure to check Chapter 4, *Going Deeper with Deep Learning*.

Multi-agent environments

It likely started out as a fun experiment, but as it turns out, letting agents compete against themselves can really amp up training, and, well, it's just cool. There are a few configurations we can set up when working with multiple agents. The `BananaCollector` example we will look at uses a single brain shared among multiple competing agents. Open up Unity and follow this exercise to set up the scene:

1. Load the `BananaCollectorBananaRL` scene file located in the `Assets/ML-Agents/Examples/BananaCollectors/` folder.

2. Leave the **Brain** on **Player**; if you changed it, change it back.

3. Run the scene in Unity. Use the **WASD** keys to move the agent cubes around the scene and collect bananas. Notice how there are multiple cubes responding identically. That is because each agent is using the same brain.

4. Expand the **RLArea** object in the **Hierarchy** window, as shown in the following screenshot:

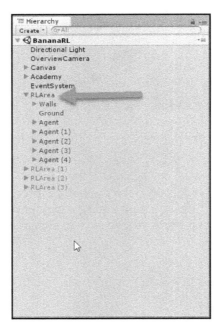

Inspecting the RLArea and agents

5. Notice the five **Agent** objects under the **RLArea**. These are the agents that will be training against the single brain. After you run the first example, you come back and duplicate more agents to test the effect this has on training.

6. Switch the **Brain** to **External**. Be sure your project is set to use an external brain (return to `Chapter 3`, *Deep Reinforcement Learning with Python* if you need to review this). If you have run an external brain with this project, you don't need any additional setup.

> There are also several environments in this example that will allow us to train with A3C, but for now, we will just use the single environment. Feel free to go back and try this example with multiple environments enabled.

7. From the menu, select **File | Build Settings....**. Uncheck any other active scenes and make sure the `BananaRL` scene is the only scene active. You may have to use the Add Open Scene button.

8. Build the environment to the `python` folder.

9. Open a Python or Anaconda prompt. Activate `ml-agents` and navigate to the `'ml-agents'` folder.

10. Run the trainer with the following code:

```
python python/learn.py python/python.exe --run-id=banana1 --train
```

11. Watch the sample run. The Unity environment window for this example is large enough so that you can see most of the activities going on. The objective of the game is for the agents to collect yellow bananas while avoiding the blue bananas. To make things interesting, the agents are able to shoot lasers in order to freeze opposing agents. This sample is shown in the following screenshot:

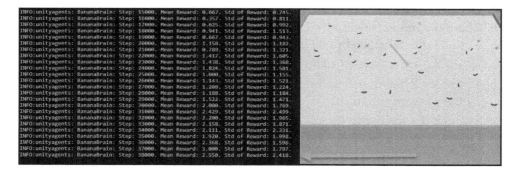

Banana Collectors multi-agent example running

You will notice that the mean and standard deviation of reward accumulates quickly in this example. This is the result of a few changes in regards to reward values for one, but this particular example is well-suited for multi-agent training. Depending on the game or simulation you are building, using multi-agents with a single brain could be an excellent way to train.

Feel free to go back and enable multiple environments in order to train multiple agents in multiple environments using multiple A3C agents. In the next section, we will look at another example that features a mix of adversarial and cooperative play using multiple agents and multiple brains.

Adversarial self-play

The last example we looked at is best defined as a competitive multi-agent training scenario where the agents are learning by competing against each other to collect bananas or freeze other agents out. In this section, we will look at another similar form of training that pits agent vs. agent using an inverse reward scheme called Adversarial self-play. Inverse rewards are used to punish an opposing agent when a competing agent receives as reward. Let's see what this looks like in the Unity ML-Agents Soccer (football) example by following this exercise:

1. Open up Unity to the `SoccerTwos` scene located in the `Assets/ML-Agents/Examples/Soccer/Scenes` folder.
2. Run the scene and use the **WASD** keys to play all four agents. Stop the scene when you are done having fun.
3. Expand the **Academy** object in the **Hierarchy** window.
4. Select the **StrikerBrain** and switch it to **External**.
5. Select the **GoalieBrain** and switch it to **External**.
6. From the menu, select **File | Build Settings....** Click the Add Open Scene button and disable other scenes so only the `SoccerTwos` scene is active.
7. Build the environment to the `python` folder.
8. Launch a Python or Anaconda prompt and activate `ml-agents`. Then, navigate to the `ml-agents` folder.
9. Launch the trainer with the following code:

```
python python/learn.py python/python.exe --run-id=soccor1 --train
```

10. Watching the training session is quite entertaining, so keep an eye on the Unity environment window and the console in order to get a sense of the training progress. Notice how the brains are using an inverse reward, as shown in the following screenshot:

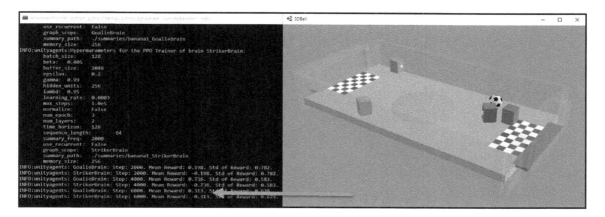

Watching the training progress of the soccer agents

The **StrikerBrain** is currently getting a negative reward and the **GoalieBrain** is getting a positive reward. Using inverse rewards allows the two brains to train to a common goal, even though they are self competing against each other as well. In the next example, we are going to look at using our trained brains in Unity as internal brains.

Using internal brains

It can be fun to train agents in multiple scenarios, but when it comes down to it, we ultimately want to be able to use these agents in a game or proper simulation. Now that we have a training scenario already set up to entertain us, let's enable it so that we can play soccer (football) against some agents. Follow this exercise to set the scene so that you can use an internal brain:

1. From the menu, select **Edit** | **Project Settings** | **Player**.

2. Enter ENABLE_TENSORFLOW in the **Scripting Define Symbols** underneath **Other Settings**, as shown in the following screenshot:

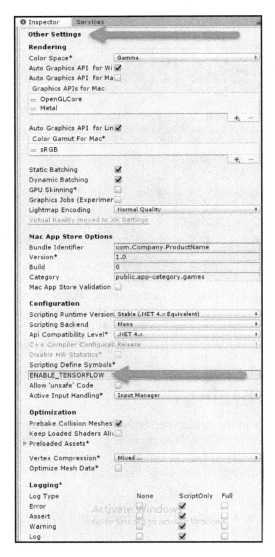

Setting the scripting define symbols for enabling TensorFlow

3. Setting this will enable the internal running of **TensorFlow** models through **TensorFlowSharp**.

4. Locate the **Academy** object and expand it to expose the **StrikerBrain** and **GoalieBrain** objects. Select the **StrikerBrain** and press *Ctrl + D* (*Command+D* on macOS) to duplicate the brain.

5. Set the original **StrikerBrain** and **GoalieBrain** to use an **Internal** brain type. When you switch the brain type, make sure that the **Graph Model** under the **TensorFlow** properties is set to **Soccer**, as shown in the following screenshot:

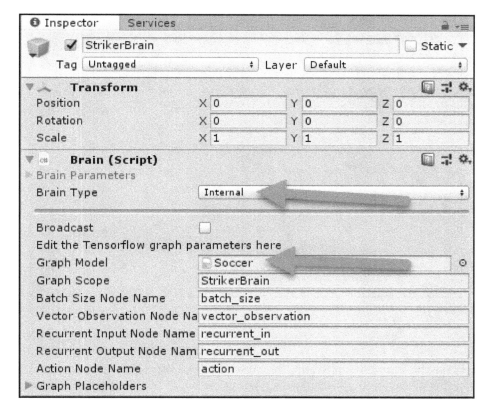

Checking that the Graph Model is set to Soccer

6. Leave the new **StrikerBrain(1)** you just duplicated to the **Player** brain type. This will allow you to play the game against the agents.

7. Expand the `SoccerFieldsTwos->Players` objects to expose the four player objects. Select the **Striker(1)** object and set its **Brain** to the **StrikerBrain(1)** player brain, as shown in the following screenshot:

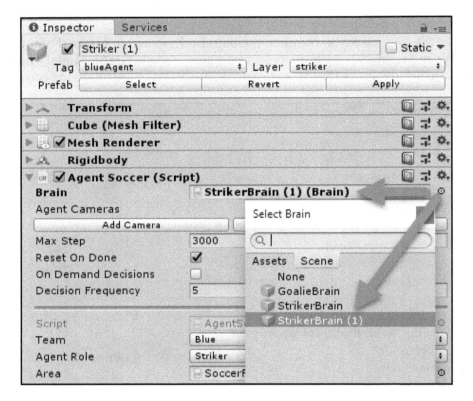

Setting the brain on the player cube

8. This sets the agent (player) to use the Player brain type we duplicated.
9. Press the **Play** button to run the game. Use the **WASD** keys to control the striker and see how well you can score. After you play for a while, you will soon start to realize how well the agents have learned.

This is a great example and quickly shows how easily you can build agents for most game scenarios given enough training time and setup. What's more is that the decision code is embedded in a light TensorFlow graph that blazes trails around other AI solutions. We are still not using new brains we have trained, so we will do that in the next section.

Using trained brains internally

In this next exercise, we want to use the brains we previously trained as agent's brains in our soccer (football) game. This will give us a good comparison to how the default Unity trained brain compares against the one we trained in our first exercise.

If you didn't complete the first exercise, go back and do that now. We are getting to the fun stuff now and you certainly don't want to miss the following exercise where we will be using a trained brain internally in a game we can play:

1. Open a **File Explorer** and open the `'ml-agents'/models/soccor1` folder. The name of the folder will match the `run-id` you used in the training command-line parameter.
2. Drag the `.bytes` file, named `python_soccer.bytes` in this example, to the `Assets/ML-Agents/Examples/Soccer/TFModels` folder, as shown in the following screenshot:

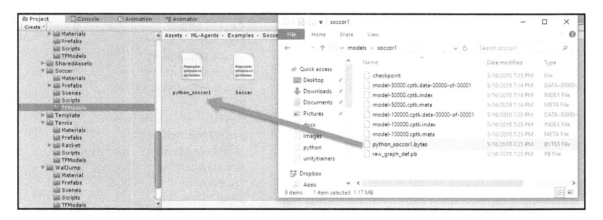

Dragging the TensorFlow model file to the TFModels folder

3. Locate the **StrikerBrain** and set the **Graph Model** by clicking the target icon and selecting the `python_soccor1` **TextAsset**, as shown in the following screenshot:

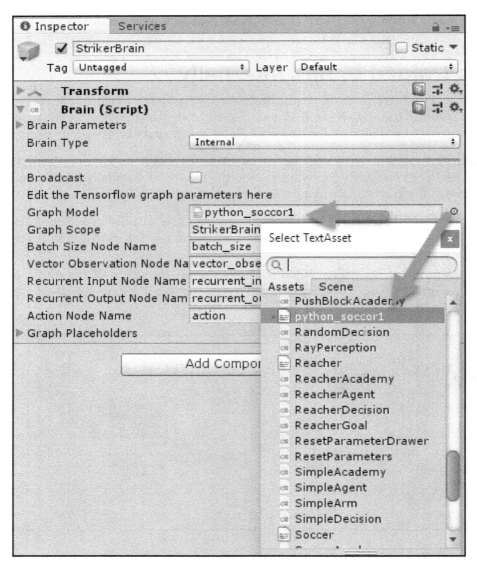

Setting the Graph Model in the StrikerBrain

4. The file is called a **TextAsset**, but it is actually a binary byte file holding the **TensorFlow** graph.

5. Change the **GoalieBrain** to the same graph model. Both brains are included in the same graph. We can denote which brain is which with the **Graph Scope** parameter. Again, leave the player striker brain as it is.

6. Press Play to run the game. Play the game with the **WASD** keys.

The first thing you will notice is that the agents don't quite play as well. That could be because we didn't use all of our training options. Now would be a good time to go back and retrain the soccer (football) brains using A3C and other options we have learned thus far.

Now that we are able to use internal brains, the training options escalate to an almost unlimited number of configurations. We will look at one interesting training method that lets our agent make on-demand decisions in the next section.

Decisions and On-Demand Decision Making

You may have noticed while playing the soccer (football) game in the previous exercise that the game went into slow motion at times. This is because the agent brains were consuming too much processing power, thus slowing the game's frame rate. This can be a problem, as we have seen from several agents running. The reason for this is that we are currently letting the agent/brains make a decision every five frames, or 1/12 second. While this is great for training, in a real game, we likely want our agents to respond at the same speed as a human would. This can remove the issue of performance since the agents now decide much less frequently. We can tune this using a feature called **On-Demand Decision Making** and **Decision Frequency**. Open up Unity to the last Soccer example we used and follow this exercise:

1. Load up the **SoccerTwos** scene from the `Assets/ML-Agents/Examples/Soccer/Scenes` folder.

2. Locate the **Players/Striker** object in the **Hierarchy** window and select it.

3. Find the **Decision Frequency** property and change it from 5, as shown in the following screenshot, to another value, up or down:

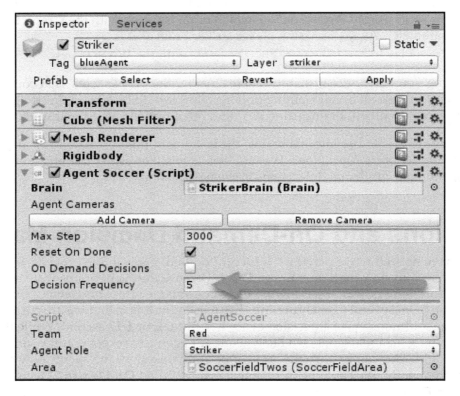

Setting the Decision Frequency to a different value

4. A value of 5 means the agent will act or decide every five frames. At 60 frames per second, this represents a reaction time of 1/12 a second or .083 seconds, which is a little quick for a person. Human reaction times can vary by age, sex, and many other factors, but for our purposes, we want to use a value of .25 to .5 seconds.

5. Set the **Decision Frequency** property to 30, as this will represent a reaction time of .5 seconds.

6. Open up the **Goalie** and **Goalie(1)** agents and set them to use a value of 30.

7. Open the **Striker(1)** agent and set its **Decision Frequency** property to 1. Remember: this is our player agent, and we don't want to hinder its reaction time, since we want to compare our own reactions to that of the agents.

8. Press the Play button to run the scene and play the game with the **WASD** keys. Do you notice anything different?

Yeah, you likely won't immediately notice any big differences. As the game plays out, you may notice that the game stays fairly fluid and doesn't slow down, but more importantly, the agents appear to react at the same speed. While we changed the reaction time to be 6x slower, the agents still appear to react at the same speed. This is mostly due to our perception of the situation, but the important take away is to train with low decision frequency and play at high decision frequency. In the next section, we will look at another technique that gives us more control on when decisions are made.

The Bouncing Banana

If you want to be more accurate in a simulation or game, you may want to set different reaction times for different input signals or events. For instance, you may only want an agent to react after it hits an object or trigger, thus not requiring the agent brain to react to a null input. Unity implemented a feature in ML-Agents called On-Demand Decision Making, which allows an agent to wait before making a decision. Unity, of course, has a sample for this, so let's open up the editor and follow this exercise:

1. Locate and open the **Bouncer** scene in the `Assets/ML-Agents/Examples/Bouncer` folder.

2. Find and select the **BouncerBrain** in the **Hierarchy** window. Set the **Brain Type** to **Internal** and make sure the **Graph Model** is set to a **TextAsset** bytes file.

3. Press the Play button to run the scene and watch the agent jump for the banana.

The last example, while quick, was a great example of **On-Demand Decision Making**. The agent in this example has the following set on the **Bouncer Agent** script, as shown in the following screenshot:

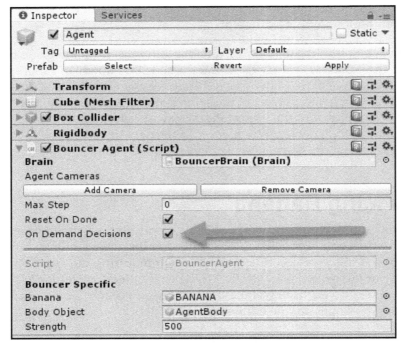

Setting an On-Demand Decision property on the Agent

When using **On-Demand Decisions,** we need to invoke a request called `RequestDecision` in our C# agent code. Let's see what this looks like by taking a close look at the `BouncerAgent` script and the `FixedUpdate` method, as shown in the following code:

```
private void FixedUpdate()
{
  if ((Physics.Raycast(transform.position, new Vector3(0f,-1f,0f), 0.51f))
    && jumpCooldown <= 0f)
  {
    RequestDecision();
    jumpLeft -= 1;
    jumpCooldown = 0.1f;
    rb.velocity = default(Vector3);
  }
  jumpCooldown -= Time.fixedDeltaTime;
  if (gameObject.transform.position.y < -1)
  {
```

```
        AddReward(-1);
        Done();
        return;
    }
    if ((gameObject.transform.localPosition.x < -19)
        ||(gameObject.transform.localPosition.x >19)
        ||  (gameObject.transform.localPosition.z < -19)
        ||  (gameObject.transform.localPosition.z > 19))
    {
    AddReward(-1);
    Done();
    return;
    }

    if (jumpLeft == 0)
    {
        Done();
    }
    bodyObject.transform.rotation =
  Quaternion.Lerp(bodyObject.transform.rotation,
    Quaternion.LookRotation(lookDir),
    Time.fixedDeltaTime * 10f);
  }
```

The first line in `FixedUpdate` checks to see if the game object is close to the floor using `Physics.Raycast` by using a downward pointing vector `(0,-1,0)` to a distance of `.51` units, making sure that the `jumpCooldown` is less than 0. When the agent gets close to the ground and has done waiting for the `jumpCooldown` time, it calls `RequestDecision()` which signals to the brain that it is time to make a decision. While the brain is set to use **On-Demand** decisions, the brain will not act until a `RequestDecision` is called.

> `FixedUpdate`, if you are less familiar with Unity, is the method that gets called for each physics time update and is tied to the physics update cycle. This is different than the `Update` method, which gets called for each render frame. The difference is subtle but you generally want to put collision detection code in `FixedUpdate`.

The rest of the code in `FixedUpdate` checks to see if the agent has fallen off the platform. If it has, then the episode resets. Otherwise, the agent will rotate in the orientation of the look direction (`lookDir`), which we set earlier in the script. If you are having trouble following the rest of the code, then you will need to brush up on your C# and Unity programming skills.

On-Demand decisions are an excellent way to both manage multiple agent's performance and give your agents more realistic behaviors. One of the things you need to keep in mind when building agents is how they actually interact with other players or, possibly, agents. Being able to tune decision frequency and timing are powerful features that we will spend more time on in `Chapter 6`, *Terrarium Revisited – A Multi-Agent Ecosystem*.

In the next section, we get back into introducing more interesting training techniques where we will train an agent by letting them imitate our actions.

Imitation learning

Imitation learning is a cool training technique that we can use to train agents by example. This has tremendous benefits in complex training scenarios with repetitive actions. Games like Pong or Tennis are very good candidates for this type of training since the game action is repetitive. Since the agent is learning by example, the need for random search actions or exploration is eliminated and training performance improves dramatically. Unity has a Tennis example that makes a good candidate to demonstrate this type of training. Let's jump to the next exercise where we set up imitation learning:

1. Open the **Tennis** scene located in the `Assets/ML-Agents/Examples/Tennis` folder.
2. Locate the **Agent** brain object in the **Hierarchy**. Rename the object `Student`. Set the **Brain Type** to **External**.
3. Select the **Player** brain object and rename it `Teacher`. Set the **Brain Type** to **Player** and make sure that the brain is set to **Broadcast**, as shown in the following screenshot:

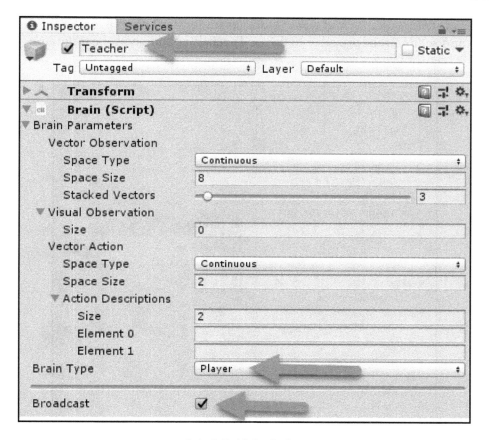

Setting the Teach brain to Broadcast

4. Setting the **Teacher** brain to **Broadcast** allows the brain to communicate with the trainer. The brain will broadcast its observations and action space to the trainer, which allows the student brain to learn from the teacher's experiences.

5. Locate the `AgentA` and `AgentB` objects under the **TennisArea**. Select either agent and set its **Brain** property to be the **Teacher**, as shown in the following screenshot:

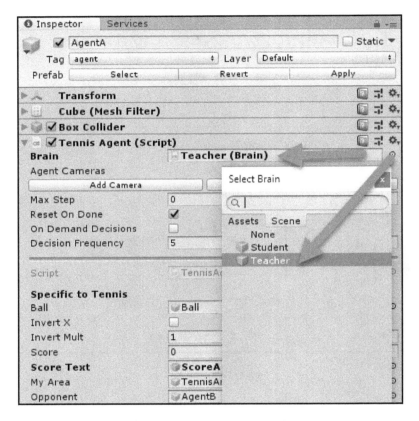

Setting AgentA to use the Teacher (player) brain

6. The **Teacher** is the brain, which you, the player, will use to teach the **Student**.
7. Locate and select the **Teacher** brain again in the **Hierarchy** window. Then, in the **Inspector** window, click the Add Component button at the bottom of the window. Search for the **BC Teacher Helper component (Script)** and add it to the object. This component will allow us to turn on/off imitation training using the **Record Key** and **Reset** experience with the **Reset Key**, as shown in the following screenshot:

Setting the BC Teacher Helper keys

8. From the menu, select **File | Build Settings....** This will open the build settings dialog. Make sure to set the Tennis scene as the only open scene and click the **Build** button.

With the scene built into our Unity environment, we now need to configure the `trainer_config.yaml` file with the proper training configuration.

Setting up a cloning behavior trainer

The trainer we use when performing Imitation Learning is called **Behavioral Cloning**. This trainer matches the **PPO** trainer we have used many times before, but it is extended to take observation and action space input from a training or player brain. Fortunately, the configuration is quite similar and only requires some special customization. Follow this exercise to finish configuring the trainer and play the game:

1. Open the `trainer_config.yaml` file in Visual Studio Code or your favorite editor and add the following new section at the end of the file:

```
Student:
    trainer: imitation
    max_steps: 10000
    summary_freq: 1000
    brain_to_imitate: Teacher
        batch_size: 16
    batches_per_epoch: 5
    num_layers: 4
        hidden_units: 64
    use_recurrent: false
    sequence_length: 16
    buffer_size: 128
```

2. The new section creates the configuration for our training brain, called **Student**. Recall that this is the brain object we renamed to **Student** earlier. We set the trainer to **imitation** from **PPO**, which is what we would normally set. The implementation of the imitation algorithm we are using is called Behavioral Cloning. **Behavioral Cloning** is the simplest form of Imitation Learning, but as you will see it, works quit handily. Save the file when you are done editing it.

3. Open a Python or Anaconda prompt and activate ml-agents and navigate to the 'ml-agents' folder.

4. Start the training session by entering the following trainer command:

```
python python/learn.py python/python.exe --run-id=tennis1 --train
--slow
```

5. Note the use of --slow. This allows the training to run in a manner that will allow us to interact with the actual environment.

6. As the environment starts, you will notice that the environment expands to a larger window and that you can control one of the agents. Use the **WASD** keys to control the agent and see how well you can return the ball. As you play the game, you should notice that many of the same moves you do, the learning agent does as well. This is a really fun way to train an agent and it makes for a pretty good time-wasting game on its own.

7. You can use the **Reset Reward (R key)** or **Reset Experience (C key)** to enable/disable training and reset experience respectively. You will also see the following key shortcuts in the environment window:

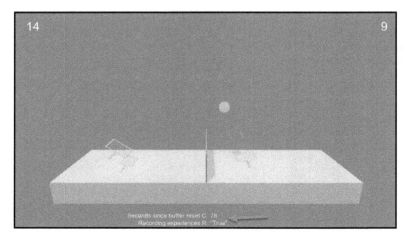

Using the Teacher brain (player) to teach the agent

8. You can try and reset the experience by pressing **C** or disabling recording experiences by typing **R**. Give them a try and see what effect these have on the agent.

As you have just seen, Imitation Learning is certainly the most fun and engaging way to train an agent. This method of training also opens up potentially endless possibilities in training game agents or agents that need to perform some memorized or redundant set of tasks, be it in games or building something more complex. As we have seen, though, even making a game where a player teaches an agent is a possibility.

In the next section, we up our training game yet again to yet more complex tasks. This time, we will look at a form of stage or curriculum training that is perfect for training agents on especially difficult multi-stage tasks.

Curriculum Learning

As you get more comfortable building agent, you will start to tackle larger problems, which are so large that it often may be better to break the task down to levels of difficulty, not unlike a game. After the problem is decomposed, it can be tackled with Curriculum Learning. Curriculum Learning is where an agent learns a task in stages or levels that increase in difficulty. It really is not unlike the way we learn a task as humans, for example, walking; we first learn to roll, then crawl, stand, stagger, and then walk. We have intuitively learned how to walk this way, but our agent friends need a bit of help, at least for now.

Let's go back to Unity and look at an example that is mostly configured for Curriculum Learning, it just needs a bit of our help to complete the setup. Follow this exercise to set up a Curriculum Learning scenario:

1. Open the `WallJump` scene in the `Assets/ML-Agents/Examples/WallJump/Scenes` folder. If you have followed all the previous exercises, you will have now worked with all the Unity example scenes and you are certainly on your way to becoming an **RL** master.

2. Select the **Academy** object in the **Hierarchy** and notice the **Reset Parameters** under the **Wall Jump Academy** component, as shown in the following screenshot:

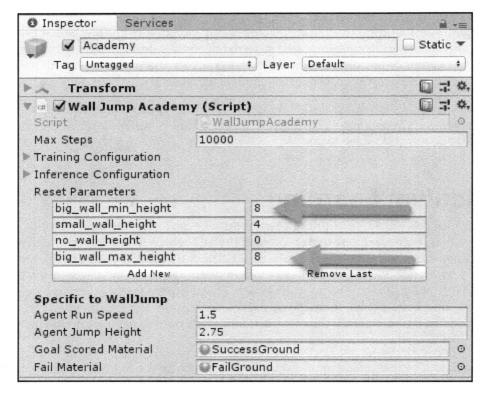

Checking the Reset Parameters on the Academy object

3. We haven't worked with these parameters too much, but they are used to define various environment variables that may change from reset to reset. In **Curriculum Learning**, we use these parameters as a way to define difficulty. In the current example, we have a parameter that defines the minimum wall height (big_wall_min_height) and maximum wall height (big_well_max_height). Our trainer will use these parameters to adjust the height of the wall during training.
4. Change the brain type to **External** on both the **SmallWallBrain** and **BigWallBrain**. You should be able to do this in your sleep by now.
5. Build the environment for external training. Again, you should know this in your sleep.

6. Open Visual Studio Code or your favorite text editor and create a new file called `curricula.json`. Save the file to the `python` folder.

7. Edit the `curricula.json` file with the following JSON:

```json
{
  "measure" : "reward",
  "thresholds" : [0.5, 0.5, 0.5, 0.5, 0.5, 0.5, 0.5, 0.5, 0.5],
  "min_lesson_length" : 2,
  "signal_smoothing" : true,
  "parameters" :   {
     "big_wall_min_height" : [0.0, 0.5, 1.0, 1.5, 2.0, 2.5, 3.0, 3.5,
     4.0, 4.5],
     "big_wall_max_height" : [4.0, 4.5, 5.0, 5.5, 6.0, 6.5, 7.0, 7.5,
     8.0, 8.5]
  }
}
```

> JSON stands for JavaScript Object Notation. While its origins are JavaScript, the notation itself is now the standard for most configuration settings. If you are not familiar with the format, learn it.

8. In this configuration (JSON) file, we are defining several parameters, which are defined as follows:

    - `measure`: Determines the process by which to measure success. The allow values are:
        - **reward**: Based on returned cumulative reward
        - **progress**: How far an agent has undertaken a task
    - `thresholds` (`array float`): Determines the points in value by which the lesson will be increased. Here, it is set to `.5` for all lessons.
    - `min_lesson_length` (`int`): Sets how many times the progress measure is reported before incrementing the lesson.

- signal_smoothing (true/false): If true, it uses a signal smoothing algorithm to blend new at .75x and old at .25x measures.
- parameters: This is where we match up the **Reset Parameters** in the **Academy** with the ranges we want the agent to train against. You will notice how the value increases by .5 for the min and max heights of the wall. In our example, this means that the wall will get increasingly higher.

9. Open a **Python** or **Anaconda** prompt and, well, you know the rest by now. Run the trainer with the following command on a single line:

```
python python/learn.py python/python.exe --run-id=walljump1 --train
--slow
--curriculum=python/curricula.json
```

10. The new parameter we are using here is --curriculum=, which points to our previously configured training file. As the training session runs, you will see that the agent takes on taller and taller walls, as shown in the following screenshot:

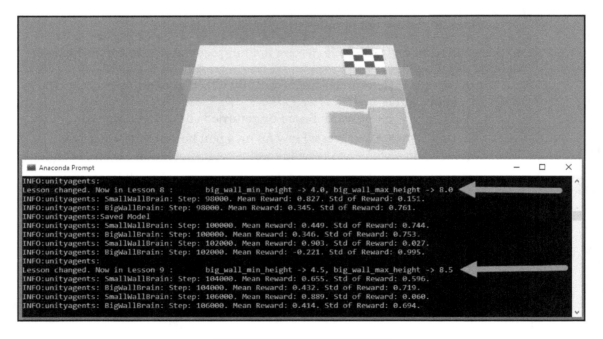

Curriculum training session running in an environment

As the agent runs, watch the prompt window as well. You will see the agent training on progressively higher and higher walls, just as the preceding excerpt shows. This form of training can be applied to all forms of situations, as we will see in `Chapter 6`, *Terrarium Revisited – A Multi-Agent Ecosystem*, where we will use Curriculum Training to cycle through various training environments, for instance.

Exercises

This chapter tried to cover a lot of material, but did not provide many practical new examples. Be sure to try some of the following exercises to build on your already growing experience as an RL guru:

1. Return to the Banana Collectors and add several more agents using *Ctrl + D* or (*Command + D* on macOS). How can you keep adding agents without the training scenario lagging or slowing down too much?

2. Convert the **Soccor** example to use Imitation Learning for one of the players. If you select the Goalie type, then set one Goalie player as a Teacher and one as a Student.

3. Convert the **GridWorld** example to use Imitation Learning. Create a new Teacher agent and convert the existing agent into a Student. We covered this example in some detail, so it will be a great comparison to the see the difference in training performance.

4. Expand on the **WallJump** example by adding additional training reset parameters. You could increase the difficultly by placing an agent farther and farther away from the wall, thus also making the agent first have to find the wall.

5. Convert the **GridWorld** example to use Curriculum Learning. You will need to create new reset parameters for the min/max values you want to set. You could increase the grid size and the number of obstacles, but decrease rewards to make more difficult training situations. See if you can best the current models.

Even doing one or two exercises is better than none at all.

Summary

This has been an exciting chapter and we have been able to play with several variations of training scenarios. We started by looking at extending our training to multi-agent environments that still used a single brain. Next, we looked at a variation of multi-agent training called Adversarial self-play, that allows us to train pairs of agents using a system of inverse rewards. Then, we covered how an agent can be configured to make decisions at a specific frequency or even on demand. After that, we looked at another novel method of training called Imitation Learning. This training scenario allowed us to play and, at the same time, teach an agent to play tennis. Finally, we completed the chapter with another training technique called Curriculum Learning, which allowed us to gradually increase the complexity of an agent's training over time.

In this chapter, we played through the last of the Unity samples and should be quite familiar with the various techniques of agent training. In the next chapter, we will build our own multi-agent world that is meant to continually evolve agents and give us the skills to apply many of these techniques on our own.

6
Terrarium Revisited – A Multi-Agent Ecosystem

In 2002, Microsoft developed a fun little developer game called Terrarium that demonstrated the code portability of the .NET Framework. Back then, C# and .NET were just newcomers and Microsoft had a tough sell; after all, it was dethroning VBA and Visual Basic as well as trying to steal away Java developers. The game allowed developers to build tiny programmable creatures that would be born, eat, sleep, reproduce, and die in a terrarium. It also featured the ability of allowing tiny programs to infect other connected terrariums. In fact, Microsoft has a contest that pitted these tiny creature programs against each other and the winning developer was the one that had the most successful creature. While we won't go so far as to build a connected terrarium infrastructure, we will do our best to replicate a number of the cooler features that made the original game so entertaining (as a developer, anyway).

The focus of this chapter will be to develop a similar terrarium game which allows our agents to live and die, but with a few twists. While neural nets and other ML technologies were available at the time, virtually all the terrarium creatures were based on A* and heuristic methods that were created by developers. Now, we have the ability to let the little terrarium creatures program themselves and develop their own winning behaviors, possibly in ways we have never even thought about. This is going to be an exciting chapter and here is what we will cover:

- What Terrarium was/is
- Building the Agent ecosystem
- Basic Terrarium – Plants and Herbivores
- Carnivore: the hunter
- Next steps
- Exercises

In this chapter, we have a lot of ground to cover and we will need to go over some advanced Unity concepts quickly. If you find yourself in trouble, download the book's source code and look at the completed example.

If the concept of growing your own little programmable creatures in a terrarium doesn't excite you, then you probably picked this book up by accident. Please give it back to its rightful owner, thanks.

What was/is Terrarium?

Terrarium was a concept that was probably ahead of its time. While the game did allow developers to transfer some form of state between parents and offspring, it was a feature that was never used in successful agents. Instead, developers just optimized their code for a particular set of fixed strategies, which in many cases turned out to be a lot of code. The following is an example screenshot of a Terrarium client running in ecosystem mode:

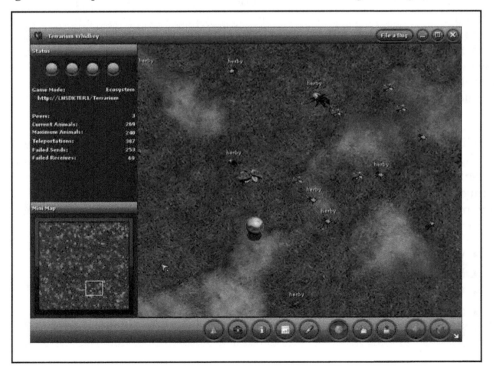

Original Microsoft Terrarium

Now, the bottom line is that we are not going to be able to replicate the entire Terrarium connected ecosystem concept in one chapter. The elegance that was the Terrarium network ecosystem infrastructure could possibly take several chapters to explain. Instead, our goal is going to build a multi-agent multi-brain ecosystem that is designed to teach you more about building an ML-Agents environment and Deep Reinforcement Learning. Perhaps someone like Microsoft or Unity will take the connected ecosystem concept further – who knows.

The Terrarium game rules were fairly simple and one of the basic rules was that your code had to run in x amount of time without failure or the creature died. There were other aspects that allowed you to apply points into a creature's abilities like size, speed, toughness, and so on that we will focus on. Developers had 100 points that they could apply to various categories for creatures of type carnivore and herbivore, as shown in the following sample tables:

Attributes	Herbivore	Carnivore	Description
Max Energy	20	10	Determines the amount of energy the creature can store for actions. Carnivores consume energy by eating other creatures. Herbivores eat plants.
Eating Speed	2	6	Determines how fast the creature can consume energy from another creature.
Attack Damage	0	14	Amount of damage another creature causes in an attack.
Defend Damage	10	10	Determines how effective a creature defends from an attack. A creature with a higher defense will inflict damage back on the attacker.
Max Speed	8	10	Determines how fast a creature moves.
Camouflage	25	5	How difficult it is to see the creature.

Eyesight	5	20	How far away a creature can detect other creatures.
Mature Size	30	20	We are adding Mature Size to the original parameters in order to hopefully make the game more balanced.
Growth Rate	5	5	This is another parameter that has been added to manage creature growth a little cleaner. The original game handled creature growth a bit like a black box.

On top of this, all creatures have a Mature Size attribute that can vary from 24 to 48, which corresponded to the icon's image size in the original game. We will map all of these attributes to various game mechanics when we build the example, but for us to perform reinforcement learning, we are going to need to apply some form of reward structure as well.

Previously, all of our rewards have been goal orientated; get to the goal and get a reward. With Terrarium however, the goal was and still is to make our agents live as long as possible and reproduce. Therefore, we want to introduce a reward system that also mimics this. We will do this by giving rewards based on the following events:

Event	Reward	Description
Die of old age	+1	Our goal will be for the creature agents to survive as long as possible.
Reproduce	+1	We want to encourage reproduction; more agents means more learning and food for others.
Eat	+energy eaten/100	We give this micro reward in order to encourage creatures to eat. Without it, they may realize they don't need to do this and just continually die of starvation. Besides, everyone enjoys eating, right?
Die of sickness	-1	In the original game, a creature died of sickness if the code crashed or the agent was unable to move. Adding this as a negative reward should hopefully reduce overcrowding.

The original game was run in real-time, but was essentially turn-based, where during each turn the agents would run through a series of events or functions based on its current state, as follows:

Event	Function
BornEvent	Fires after a creature is born.
LoadEvent	Fires after a creature has been loaded into the environment.
IdleEvent	Fires when the agent needs to make a decision, we can essentially convert that to use on-demand decisions.
ReproduceCompletedEvent	Fires after an agent reproduces; this will be a reward event for our purposes.
EatCompletedEvent	Fires after an agent eats. Again, another opportunity to give rewards.
DefendCompletedEvent	Agents need to explicitly perform a defensive action. This event will fire after an agent defends itself.
AttackCompletedEvent	Fires when an agent finishes attacking.
AttackedEvent	Fires after a creature is attacked.
MoveCompletedEvent	Fires after an agent moves.

Now, in the original game, it was the job of the developer to implement their own code in each of the preceding events in order to control the agent. For our purposes, we will use a real-time physics-based system that will activate these events based on agent timing. Each action an agent performs will take some amount of time determined by the creature's speed or eating speed. This is why it is critical that an agent can move and consume resources (other creatures) quickly.

During a turn, an agent can perform the following actions:

Action	Description
Wait	A creature can wait and stay idle, thus conserving energy.
Move	Movement consumes `.01` x creature's current size in energy per movement action.
Attack	Attacking consumes `.01` x creature's size in energy. An attack scores damage equal to the attack strength multiplied by the creature size, subtracting any defending creatures defense x creature size. If a herbivore is not defending, the attacker strikes at full damage.
Defend	Defending consumes `.005` x creature's size in energy. A creature must explicitly defend itself in order to block an attack.
Eat	Eating consumes energy at the rate of its eating speed per time scale. A creature cannot eat an active herbivore or carnivore, but may eat living plants.
Reproduce	Reproduction consumes 1/2 the creature's energy. In order to reproduce, the creature must have greater than 50% of its maximum energy and be of mature size.

In addition to the preceding actions, a creature will also undergo various transformations as it grows and dies, as shown in the following table:

Lifetime Event	Description
Born	Spawning a new creature will happen whenever a grown creature has reached its maximum size and has an energy surplus, `energy > max energy + 1`.
Grow	A creature will grow any time its energy level has increased by 50%. A growth spurt will immediately reduce a creature's current energy by 25%. If you want, you could also add a micro reward here to encourage creature growth.
Die of old age	The creature has lived as long as its lifespan allows. A creature's lifespan is set by its size, so larger creatures live longer.
Die of starvation or sickness	The creature exhausts all of its `energy < 0` and dies. A creature with 0 energy could live idle into old age, but if it tries to move, defend, or attack, it will die. It is conceivable that another creature could bring it food, but we shall see how that plays out.
Killed	When a creature is killed by another creature, it dies but is not destroyed. The dead creature is left with max energy for carnivore creatures to consume.

The preceding lifetime events will occur automatically as the agent lives and will be controlled by the Academy object that we will develop to control the training scenario. With all of those rules out of the way, we can continue to build an agent Terrarium in the next section.

Building the Agent ecosystem

Now that we have a core set of rules, we can start to build our multi-agent ecosystem from scratch in Unity. Previously, we spent a considerable amount of time looking at the Unity canned samples, but that was essential in order to cover all the material to get to this point in such a short time. With all the core understanding out of the way, we can now build a more complex example by following this exercise:

1. From the **Project** window, create a new folder called `Terrarium` under `Assets`.
2. Create five new folders called `Materials`, `Prefabs`, `Scenes`, `Scripts`, and `TFModels`.
3. Create a new scene called `Terrarium` in the `Scenes` folder.
4. Open the new **Terrarium** scene and from the menu, select `GameObject ->` `Create Empty`. Rename the object to `Academy`.
5. Open the `Scripts` folder in the **Project** window. Create a new C# script called `TerrariumAcademy`. Edit the script so that it contains the following code:

```
using UnityEngine;
  public class TerrariumAcademy : Academy {
    public override void AcademyReset() {
    }
    public override void AcademyStep() {
    }
  }
```

6. We won't need much code because we are extending from the standard ML-Agents **Academy** script. Save the script when you're done editing it and return to Unity. Wait for the scripts to compile with no errors.

7. Drag the **TerrariumAcademy** script onto the **Academy** object to attach it as a component. Set the **Terrarium Academy** component parameters as follows:

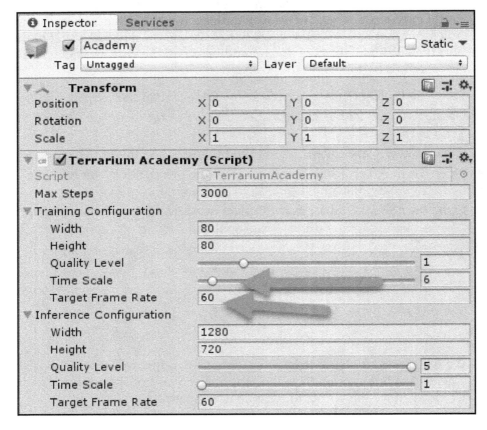

Setting the Academy training configuration parameters

8. Setting these parameters will make sure that we can run the training session using the trainer parameter `--slow` and see the simulation run.

This sets up the first part of our project, but we have several more steps to do. In the next section, we will import some colorful assets to make our Terrarium a little more fun.

Importing Unity assets

One of the most compelling aspects of Unity is the Asset Store. There resides so much quality content on the store that you could literally develop an entire game without any code. Of course, we won't have that luxury, but we will take advantage of the many free assets to spice up our Terrarium. Open Unity back up and follow along to import the project assets:

1. From the menu, select **Window** | **Asset Store**. The **Asset Store** is currently in transition at the time of writing and some screenshots may look quite different or the assets will be gone. Either way, any low polygon creature or animal pack will do.

2. Enter the search text `gloomy animal` in the search bar and click search or hit enter. You will see a few search results appear. Select the asset called the `Free Low_Polygon Animal` pack, as shown in the following screenshot:

Importing the low polygon animal pack

3. Click **Download** and then the **Import** button, as shown in the preceding screenshot. This will import the asset into the project. You will be prompted to select which assets to import. Make sure that all of the items are selected, and then click **Import** on the import dialog.

4. Go back to the **Asset Store** window and search for `low poly toon`. Select the asset, as shown in the following screenshot:

Importing the low poly toon asset into the project

5. Download and import the asset into the project.

Unity has a broad and varied selection of excellent and not so excellent assets. Be careful because not all paid assets may be what they seem and may often cause you more grief. Likewise, there are a number of excellent free assets, like the ones we are using, but there are also plenty of not so good free assets. If you are investing any time or money on an asset, be sure it works for you and your project. Many a project has suffered from asset bloat because it seemed like a good idea at the time. Remember, even free assets have a price: time.

With our new assets imported, we can work towards adding the environment to our project in the next section.

Building the environment

The original Terrarium game was in 2D, because that was easier at the time, but now it's actually easier for us to make our version in 3D. Aside from that improvement, we will be using the poly animals and plants instead of 2D icons. First, we will need to build our world by following this exercise:

1. Load up the **Terrarium** scene.
2. From the menu, select **GameObject** | **Create Empty**. Rename the new object **Environment**.
3. Right-click (*Command* click on macOS) the new **Environment** object and from the context menu, select **3D Object** | **Plane**. Reset the plane's position to 0, 0, 0 if need be. Set the **Transform** | **Scale** to (5, 1, 5).
4. Select the new **Plane** object in the **Hierarchy** window and then change the **Material** property of the **Mesh Renderer** component to brown_01, as shown in the following screenshot:

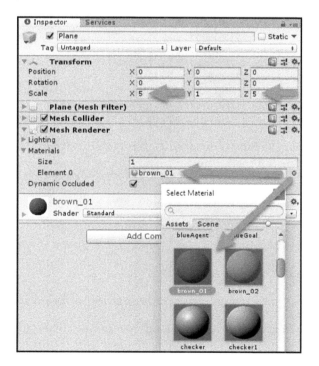

Changing the plane's render material

5. Create a new script called `LookCamera` in the Scripts folder and edit the contents to look as follows:

```
using UnityEngine;
using System.Collections;

public class LookCamera : MonoBehaviour
{
  public float mouseSensitivityX = 5.0f;
  public float mouseSensitivityY = 5.0f;

  float rotY = 0.0f;

  void Start()
  {
    if (GetComponent<Rigidbody>())
      GetComponent<Rigidbody>().freezeRotation = true;
  }
  void Update()
  {
    if (Input.GetMouseButton(1))
    {
      float rotX = transform.localEulerAngles.y +
      Input.GetAxis("Mouse X") *
      mouseSensitivityX;
      rotY += Input.GetAxis("Mouse Y") * mouseSensitivityY;
      rotY = Mathf.Clamp(rotY, -89.5f, 89.5f);
      transform.localEulerAngles = new Vector3(-rotY, rotX, 0.0f);
    }
    if (Input.GetKey(KeyCode.W) || Input.GetKey(KeyCode.UpArrow))
    {
      transform.position += transform.forward * .1f;
    }
    else if (Input.GetKey(KeyCode.S) ||
    Input.GetKey(KeyCode.DownArrow))
    {
      transform.position -= transform.forward * .1f;
    }
    if (Input.GetKey(KeyCode.U))
    {
      gameObject.transform.localPosition = new Vector3(0.0f, 50.0f,
      0.0f);
      transform.localEulerAngles = new Vector3(90f, 0.0f, 0.0f);
    }
  }
}
```

6. This is a basic **LookCamera** script that allows you to freely move and rotate the camera through the scene. There are plenty of variations of this script free online if you want additional features. Read the script in order to figure out the controls and the special reset key.

7. Attach the **LookCamera** script to the scene's **Main Camera** and modify the objects properties in the **Inspector** as follows:

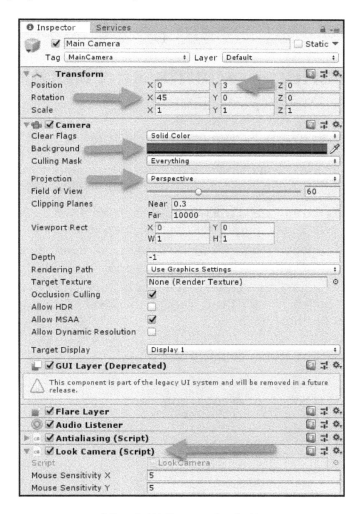

Setting up the Main Camera properties and scripts

8. Press the play button to run the scene. Use the **LookCamera** script input controls to move the camera around the scene. Try pressing the special key to see what happens; read the script again if you're not sure what keys do what. The current version of this script is unbounded, meaning you can go anywhere. Feel free to add your own bounding box that restricts the camera.

Now that we have our basic agent environment set up, we want to jump in and tackle adding plants and animals in the next section.

Basic Terrarium – Plants and Herbivores

The bulk of our work in setting up our terrarium is going to be building the plants, agents that eat plants (herbivores), and agents that eat agents that eat plants (carnivores). We will start with our most basic form of terrarium inhabitant, the plant. Terrarium plants are not unlike their natural cousins; they continually increase in energy by just existing. When they reach a certain size, they also begin discharging seeds that produce more plants and so on. Open up Unity and follow along to create our first Terrarium inhabitant, the plant:

1. Open the Terrarium scene where we last left it and from the menu select **GameObject | Create Empty**. Rename the new object `Plant`.
2. Drag the `Plant` object onto the `Environment -> Plane` to attach it as a child. Make sure to reset the `Transform Position` to `(0,0,0)`.
3. Open the `Assets/Free Low Poly Toon Nature/Prefabs` folder and drag the `tree_F08` prefab onto the **Plant** object in the scene. Make sure the child prefab's **Transform Position** is `0,0,0`.
4. Create a new **C#** script in the `Assets/Terrarium/Scripts` folder and call it **Plant**. Open the script in your editor of choice and replace it with:

```
using UnityEngine;
public class Plant : MonoBehaviour {
  [Header("Plant Points (30 Max)")]
  public float MaxEnergy;
  public float MatureSize;
  public float GrowthRate;
  public float SeedSpreadRadius;

  [Header("Monitoring")]
  public float Energy;
  public float Size;
  public float Age;
```

```
[Header("Seedling")]
public GameObject SeedlingSpawn;

[Header("Species Parameters")]
public float EnergyGrowthRate = .01f;
public float AgeRate = .001f;
private Transform Environment;
private void Start()
{
  Size = 1;
  Energy = 1;
  Age = 0;
  Environment = transform.parent;
  TransformSize();
}

void Update ()
{
  if (CanGrow) Grow();
  if (CanReproduce) Reproduce();
  if (Dead) Destroy(this);
  Age += AgeRate;
  Energy += EnergyGrowthRate;
}

void TransformSize()
{
  transform.localScale = Vector3.one * Size;
}

bool CanGrow
{
  get
  {
    return Energy > ((MaxEnergy / 2) + 1);
  }
}

bool CanReproduce
{
  get
  {
    if (Size >= MatureSize && CanGrow) return true;
    else return false;
  }
}

bool Dead
```

```
{
  get
  {
    return Energy < 0 || Age > MatureSize;
  }
}

void Grow()
{
  if (Size > MatureSize) return;
  Energy = Energy / 2;
  Size += GrowthRate * Random.value;
  TransformSize();
}

 void Reproduce()
 {
   var vec = Random.insideUnitCircle * SeedSpreadRadius + new
   Vector2(transform.position.x, transform.position.z);
   Instantiate(SeedlingSpawn, new Vector3(vec.x,0,vec.y),
   Quaternion.identity,
   Environment);
   Energy = Energy / 2;
 }
}
```

5. For the most part, the preceding code should be straightforward enough to follow; we will take a closer look at the **Reproduce** method later. Those of you new to Unity should remember that **Start** is called when the object starts up and **Update** is called every rendering frame. If you take a look at the **Update** method in more detail, you will see the whole life cycle of the plant. The sections we have for the various editor fields want to expose and use the **Header** attribute. Save the script when you are done editing it and return to Unity, making sure no compiler errors appear.

6. Attach the **Plant** script to the **Plant** object. You can do this by dragging the script or using **Add Component**; it's your choice. While you are at it, also add a **Rigid Body** and **Capsule Collider** components as well. Edit the properties of the various script components so that they match the following screenshot:

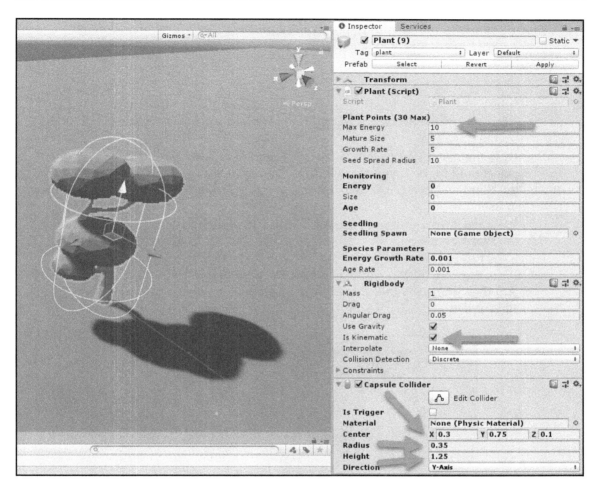

Setting the Plant component properties

7. Open your code editor to the **Plant** script and scroll down to the **Reproduce** method. When this method is called, the plant spawns new seedlings with the call to **Instantiate**. **Instantiate** creates new game objects in the scene based on a template object called a **prefab** in Unity. Prefabs are a cornerstone in Unity development and create reusable objects for all forms of development activities.

The next part is tricky and may require your full attention. If you get frustrated, take a look at this example in the book's source code.

8. Select and drag the **Plant** object from the **Hierarchy** window to the **Assets/Terrarium/Prefabs** folder in the **Project** window to create a new **Plant** prefab.

9. Drag the new **Plant** prefab and drop it onto the **Plant - Seedling Spawn** game object field in the **Inspector** window. This creates a recursive relationship with the **Plant** and itself or spawn, meaning that the **Plant** will always spawn a copy of itself.

10. Press the **Apply** button in the **Prefab** section at the top of the window to update the **Plant** prefab with the recursive relationship. With a single plant in our terrarium, we can now go ahead and run an example.

11. Press the Play button and watch how the plant becomes multiple plants in time and then gradually takes over the terrarium, as shown in the following screenshot:

Plants overgrowing in the terrarium

At this point, you can use the single plant we just made or go back and create other plant types using the poly toon nature prefabs we downloaded. If you do, make sure that you vary the points you give to each of the new species of plants.

Now that we have established that we have a plant problem, which in our case is a good thing, since our first creature agent, the herbivore, will need to consume plants in order to survive, we will tackle building the herbivore in the next section.

Herbivores to the rescue

The herbivore will be our most basic agent that will learn to live in the terrarium. A herbivore creature will thrive by consuming plants, which will give them energy to grow and reproduce. We can follow several of the same basic patterns we used building the Plant script when creating our Herbivore agent script. Open up Unity and follow this exercise to code the Herbivore agent script:

1. Create a new script called `CreatureAgent` in the `Assets/Terrarium/Scripts` folder and open it in your editor of choice. Fortunately, we won't need to create a different script for each different type of agent if we generalize things into a single `CreatureAgent` script.

2. We will cover each section of this script as we build it. Enter the following lines of code:

```
using UnityEngine;
public enum CreatureType
{
   Herbivore,
   Carnivore
}
public class CreatureAgent : Agent
{
 [Header("Creature Type")]
 public CreatureType CreatureType;
 [Header("Creature Points (100 Max)")]
 public float MaxEnergy;
 public float MatureSize;
 public float GrowthRate;
 public float EatingSpeed;
 public float MaxSpeed;
 public float AttackDamage;
 public float DefendDamage;
 public float Eyesight;

 [Header("Monitoring")]
 public float Energy;
 public float Size;
 public float Age;
 public string currentAction;

 [Header("Child")]
 public GameObject ChildSpawn;

 [Header("Species Parameters")]
```

```
public float AgeRate = .001f;
private GameObject Environment;
private Rigidbody agentRB;
private float nextAction;
private bool died;
private RayPerception rayPer;
//private TerrariumAcademy academy;
private int count;
private Vector2 bounds;

private void Awake()
{
AgentReset();
}
```

3. All of the preceding code is mostly public and private fields, but notice the **CreatureType** enumeration at the start. Setting the type of creature will also control special logic that is specific to different creature types. You could, of course, add other creature types later. Then, we will extend **CreatureAgent** from **Agent**, since we want the **Academy** to automatically register and control this agent. At the end is the `Awake` method, which is called when the object starts up and will take care of resetting the agent.

4. Next, we will add all the methods we need to override an **Agent**, as follows:

```
public override void AgentReset()
{
  Size = 1;
  Energy = 1;
  Age = 0;
  bounds = GetEnvironmentBounds();
  var x = Random.Range(-bounds.x, bounds.x);
  var z = Random.Range(-bounds.y, bounds.y);
  transform.position = new Vector3(x, 1, z);
  TransformSize();
  InitializeAgent();
}

public override void AgentOnDone()
{}

public override void InitializeAgent()
{
  base.InitializeAgent();
  rayPer = GetComponent<RayPerception>();
  agentRB = GetComponent<Rigidbody>();
  currentAction = "Idle";
```

```
}

public override void CollectObservations()
{
  float rayDistance = Eyesight;
  float[] rayAngles = { 20f, 90f, 160f, 45f, 135f, 70f, 110f };
  string[] detectableObjects = { "plant", "herbivore", "carnivore" };
  AddVectorObs(rayPer.Perceive(rayDistance, rayAngles,
  detectableObjects, 0f, 0f));
  Vector3 localVelocity =
  transform.InverseTransformDirection(agentRB.velocity);
  AddVectorObs(localVelocity.x);
  AddVectorObs(localVelocity.z);
  AddVectorObs(Energy);
  AddVectorObs(Size);
  AddVectorObs(Age);
  AddVectorObs(Float(CanEat));
  AddVectorObs(Float(CanReproduce));
}

private float Float(bool val)
{
  if (val) return 1.0f;
  else return 0.0f;
}

public override void AgentAction(float[] vectorAction,
string textAction)
{
  //Action Space 7 float
  // 0 = Move
  // 1 = Eat
  // 2 = Reproduce
  // 3 = Attack
  // 4 = Defend
  // 5 = move orders
  // 6 = rotation
  if (vectorAction[0] > .5)
  {
    MoveAgent(vectorAction);
  }
  else if (vectorAction[1] > .5)
  {
    Eat();
  }
  else if (vectorAction[2] > .5)
  {
    Reproduce();
```

```
    }
    else if (vectorAction[3] > .5)
    {
      //Attack();
    }
    else if (vectorAction[4] > .5)
    {
      //Defend();
    }
  }
```

5. A couple of important things to note about the preceding code is the CollectObservations and AgentAction methods. CollectObservations is where we collect the agent's state using techniques that we have seen before. In AgentAction, we are checking the seven possible action values to determine what action the agent will take after a decision is made.

6. Next, we will add the Update and FixedUpate methods, as follows:

```
void Update()
{
  if (OutOfBounds)
  {
    AddReward(-1f);
    Done();
    return;
  }
  if (Buried)
  {
    Done();
  }
  if (Dead) return;
  if (CanGrow) Grow();
  if (CanReproduce) Reproduce();
  Age += AgeRate;
  MonitorLog();
}

public void FixedUpdate()
{
  if (Time.timeSinceLevelLoad > nextAction)
  {
    currentAction = "Deciding";
    RequestDecision();
  }
}
```

7. The `Update` method is similar to the `Plant Update` method and just covers the agent's life cycle. The `FixedUpdate` method checks continually to see if the agent is ready to make another decision. Recall that we do this as a way to simulate decision-making time and improve our simulation performance using on-demand decision-making using the call to `RequestDecsion`.

8. Next, we add another method called `MonitorLog` that will allow us to visualize our creature's stats as they live. Enter the following code:

```
public void MonitorLog()
{
  Monitor.Log("Action", currentAction, MonitorType.text, transform);
  Monitor.Log("Size", Size / MatureSize, MonitorType.slider,
  transform);
  Monitor.Log("Energy", Energy / MaxEnergy, MonitorType.slider,
  transform);
  Monitor.Log("Age", Age / MatureSize, MonitorType.slider,
  transform);
}
```

9. The Unity team provide us with a nice way to quickly view stats about our agents with the `Monitor.Log`. Check the Unity documents for more information on how to use this monitoring feature.

10. Finally, we are going to dump in the rest of the code, as follows:

```
public bool OutOfBounds
{
get
  {
    if (transform.position.y < 0) return true;
    if (transform.position.x > bounds.x || transform.position.x
    < -bounds.x ||              transform.position.y > bounds.y ||
    transform.position.y < -bounds.y) return
    true;
    else return false;
  }
}
void TransformSize()
{
  transform.localScale = Vector3.one * Mathf.Pow(Size,1/2);
}

bool CanGrow
{
  get
  {
```

```
      return Energy > ((MaxEnergy / 2) + 1);
  }
}

bool CanEat
{
  get
  {
    if(CreatureType == CreatureType.Herbivore)
    {
      if (FirstAdjacent("plant") != null) return true;
    }
    return false;
  }
}

private GameObject FirstAdjacent(string tag)
{
  var colliders = Physics.OverlapSphere(transform.position, 1.2f *
  Size);
  foreach (var collider in colliders)
  {
    if (collider.gameObject.tag == tag)
    {
      return collider.gameObject;
    }
  }
    return null;
}

bool CanReproduce
{
  get
  {
    if (Size >= MatureSize && CanGrow) return true;
    else return false;
  }
}

bool Dead
{
  get
  {
    if (died) return true;
    if (Age > MatureSize )
    {
      currentAction = "Dead";
      died = true;
```

```
        Energy = Size; //creature size is converted to energy
        AddReward(.2f);
        Done();
        return true;
      }
    return false;
    }
}

bool Buried
{
  get
  {
    Energy -= AgeRate;
    return Energy < 0;
  }
}

void Grow()
{
  if (Size > MatureSize) return;
  Energy = Energy / 2;
  Size += GrowthRate * Random.value;
  nextAction = Time.timeSinceLevelLoad + (25 / MaxSpeed);
  currentAction ="Growing";
  TransformSize();
}
void Reproduce()
{
  if (CanReproduce)
  {
    var vec = Random.insideUnitCircle * 5;
    var go = Instantiate(ChildSpawn, new Vector3(vec.x, 0, vec.y),
    Quaternion.identity, Environment.transform);
    go.name = go.name + (count++).ToString();
    var ca = go.GetComponent<CreatureAgent>();
    ca.AgentReset();
    Energy = Energy / 2;
    AddReward(.2f);
    currentAction ="Reproducing";
    nextAction = Time.timeSinceLevelLoad + (25 / MaxSpeed);
  }
}

public void Eat()
{
  if (CreatureType == CreatureType.Herbivore)
  {
```

```
        var adj = FirstAdjacent("plant");
        if (adj != null)
        {
          var creature = adj.GetComponent<Plant>();
          var consume = Mathf.Min(creature.Energy, 5);
          creature.Energy -= consume;
          if (creature.Energy < .1) Destroy(adj);
          Energy += consume;
          AddReward(.1f);
          nextAction = Time.timeSinceLevelLoad + (25 / EatingSpeed);
          currentAction = "Eating";
        }
      }
    }

    public void MoveAgent(float[] act)
    {
      Vector3 rotateDir = Vector3.zero;
      rotateDir = transform.up * Mathf.Clamp(act[6], -1f, 1f);
      if(act[5] > .5f)
      {
        transform.position = transform.position + transform.forward;
      }
      Energy -= .01f;
      transform.Rotate(rotateDir, Time.fixedDeltaTime * MaxSpeed);
      currentAction = "Moving";
      nextAction = Time.timeSinceLevelLoad + (25 / MaxSpeed);
    }
    private Vector2 GetEnvironmentBounds()
    {
      Environment = transform.parent.gameObject;
      var xs = Environment.transform.localScale.x;
      var zs = Environment.transform.localScale.z;
      return new Vector2(xs, zs) * 10;
    }
```

This is a big chunk of code, and while it may seem daunting, it is all relatively straightforward. That isn't all the code we will need, but it will do for now.

11. The `MoveAgent` method was borrowed from the Unity samples, so it may be familiar; the difference is that the physics code was removed to keep things simpler. The **Eat** and `FirstAdjacent` methods are where all the action happens. When a creature decides to eat and it is of type `Herbivore`, it will look for the first adjacent object, one that its collider is colliding with. If it detects an adjacent object that is of type `'plant'`, it happily eats. The `FirstAdjacent` method is the collision detection which uses a `SphereCast` to determine any adjacent objects.

12. Save the script and return to Unity to make sure that there are no compiler errors.

That completes the Herbivore part of our `CreatureAgent` script. Do go over and read the code so that you have a good idea of how it works. In the next section, we will add the Herbivore creature to the scene and start training.

Building the herbivore

In the 2002 version of Terrarium, developers had to code the brain on their own and this sometimes grew to thousands of lines of code. We, however, know that with the ML-Agents tools, we can let the creature program or build its own best solution using DRL. Open up Unity to the Terrarium scene and follow along in order to build the herbivore:

1. Right-click (*Command* click on macOS) the **Academy** object in the **Hierarchy** window. From the context menu, select **Create Empty**. Rename the new object `HerbivoreBrain`.

2. Add a **Brain** component to the object and set the properties as follows:

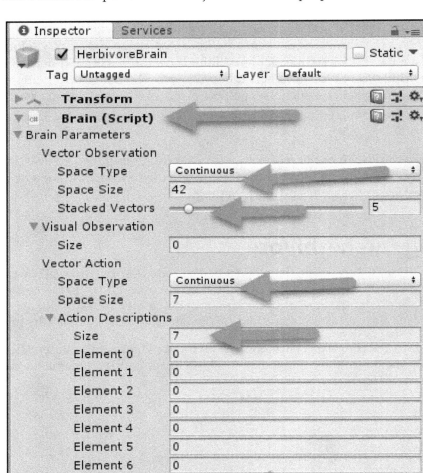

Setting the HerbivoreBrain properties

3. Create a new empty object off the **Environment** object and name it Herbivore.
4. Drag the **Chicken** model from the Assets/_Gloomy_Animal/Meshes folder and drop it as a child of the **Herbivore** object in the **Hierarchy** window.

5. Add a **Box Collider**, **Rigid Body**, and **Ray Perception** components to the **Herbivore** object and configure, them as shown in the following screenshot:

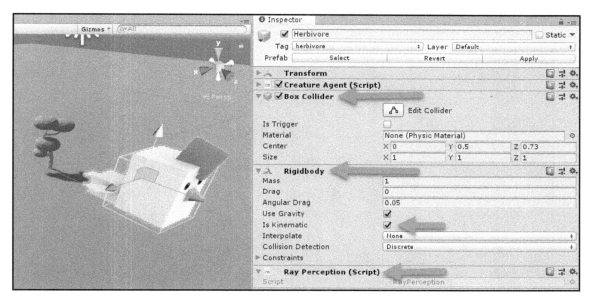

Introducing the chicken to the rules of physics

6. This will introduce the chicken to the rules of physics. We are using the **Kinematic** setting for this version in order to keep things simple. Our use of physics in this version is to make our life simpler in determining if objects are next to each other.

 In 3Dology speak, Kinematic is another way of saying fixed or stationary in the physical simulation. The object can, of course, be moved in code or out of the Unity physical realm.

7. Continuing with physics, click the **Tag** dropdown at the top of the **Inspector** window and create new **herbivore**, **carnivore**, and **plant** tags. Set the **herbivore** tag to on, as shown in the following screenshot:

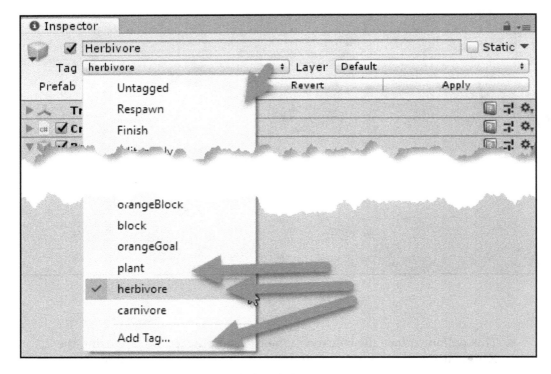

Adding the tags for the creatures

8. Tags are used in the physics engine to quickly filter by object types. If we didn't do this, most physics queries would need to run over the entire list of objects for every check, which is not very efficient.

9. Add the **CreatureAgent** script to the **Herbivore** and set the properties to those that are shown in the following screenshot:

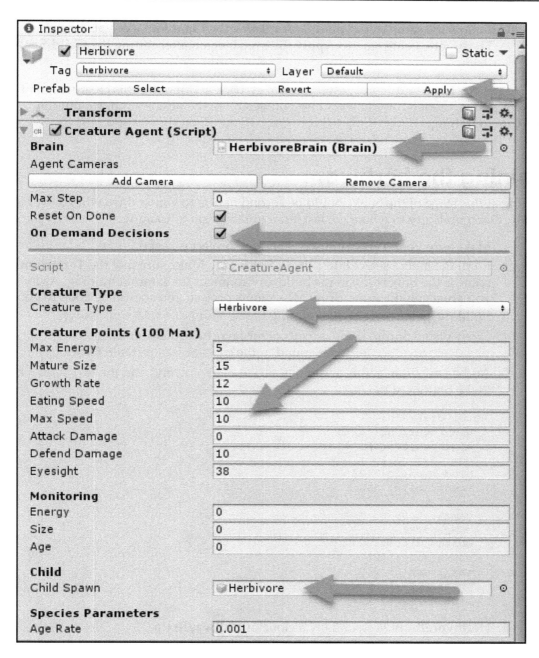

Setting the Creature Agent component properties

10. Follow the same steps you did for turning the **Plant** into a prefab for the **Herbivore**, being sure to **Apply** the prefab again after setting the **Child Spawn** to itself.

That creates the basic herbivore. Now, you can go back and modify this creature later to try different points, models, or whatever else you desire. In the next section, we put the herbivore to training.

Training the herbivore

Training at this stage of the book should be second nature to you and we will go over it quickly. Open up Unity to where we last left it and let's get to training:

1. Make sure your **Terrarium** scene and the project is saved.
2. From the menu, select **File | Build Settings...**. Make sure that the **Terrarium** scene is the only scene in the build environment for external training. As long as you are using the same Unity ML-Agents project, you should be good to go.
3. Build the game for external training to the `'python'` folder, as always.
4. Open Visual Studio Code or your other favorite text editor to the `trainer_config.yaml` file found in the `ml-agents/python` folder.
5. Add a new brain configuration, `HerbivoreBrain`, and add the text shown here to the bottom of the file:

```
HerbivoreBrain:
    use_recurrent: true
    sequence_length: 64
    num_layers: 1
    hidden_units: 128
    memory_size: 512
    beta: 1.0e-2
    gamma: 0.99
    num_epoch: 3
    buffer_size: 1024
    batch_size: 128
    max_steps: 5.0e5
    summary_freq: 500
    time_horizon: 128
```

6. **HerbivoreBrain** is essentially a clone of **HallwayBrain**.

7. Open your Python or Anaconda prompt and activate `ml-agents`. Then, do the same with the `cd ml-agents` folder.

8. Run the trainer with the following command:

```
python python/learn.py python/python.exe --run-id=terrarium1 --train
--slow
```

9. Use the **LookCamera**, and those special keys, to move around the scene as the herbivore creatures train. The following is a screenshot showing several chickens and plants in a terrarium:

Looks like we now have a chicken (herbivore) problem

Depending on how fast you let your plants grow, you could see a real big chicken problem happen quickly. Watch what happens as the herbivores expand and quickly eat themselves into extinction. This would also happen in nature if it weren't for other checks and balances, such as carnivores, disasters, and so on. We will look at adding more natural life balance to the terrarium in the next section when we add carnivores.

Carnivore: the hunter

Trying to find the balance in creating a thriving world was one of the challenges you originally faced in the original terrarium. In fact, the most challenging creature to write was no surprise: the carnivore. The carnivore is at the top of the food chain and its purpose is to consume herbivores. Not unlike the real world, this will actually help in our training of both agents. In order to add our carnivore creature, we will first need to add some code to our `CreatureAgent` script. Follow this exercise to modify the `CreatureAgent` script for carnivores:

1. Open the `CreatureAgent` script in your favorite coding editor.
2. Modify the `AgentAction` method and uncomment the **Attack** and **Defend** actions as follows:

```
public override void AgentAction(float[] vectorAction,
string textAction) {
  //Action Space 7 float
  // 0 = Move
  // 1 = Eat
  // 2 = Reproduce
  // 3 = Attack
  // 4 = Defend
  // 5 = move orders
  // 6 = rotation
  if (vectorAction[0] > .5)
  {
    MoveAgent(vectorAction);
  }
  else if (vectorAction[1] > .5)
  {
    Eat();
  }
  else if (vectorAction[2] > .5)
  {
    Reproduce();
  }
  else if (vectorAction[3] > .5)
  {
    Attack();
  }
  else if (vectorAction[4] > .5)
  {
    Defend();
  }
}
```

3. Next, the `Attack` method needs to handle attack and defense actions for both creatures. Code up the Attack method as follows:

```
void Attack()
{
  float damage = 0f;
  currentAction = "Attack";
  nextAction = Time.timeSinceLevelLoad + (25 / MaxSpeed);
  var vic = FirstAdjacent("herbivore").GetComponent<CreatureAgent>();
  if (vic != null)
  {
    if (vic.currentAction == "Defend")
    {
      damage = ((AttackDamage * Size) - (vic.DefendDamage *
      vic.Size)) / (Size *
      vic.Size);
    }
    else
    {
      damage = ((AttackDamage * Size) - (1 * vic.Size)) / (Size *
      vic.Size);
    }
  } else {
    vic = FirstAdjacent("carnivore").GetComponent<CreatureAgent>();
    if (vic != null)
    {
      if (vic.currentAction == "Attack")
      {
        damage = ((AttackDamage * Size) - (vic.AttackDamage *
        vic.Size)) / (Size
        * vic.Size);
      } else {
        damage = ((AttackDamage * Size) - (vic.DefendDamage
        * vic.Size)) /
        (Size * vic.Size);
      }
    }
  }
  if(damage > 0)
  {
    vic.Energy -= damage;
    if (vic.Energy < 0)
    { AddReward(.25f); }
  } else if(damage < 0) {
    Energy -= damage;
```

```
  }
  Energy -= .1f;
}
```

4. Most of the preceding logic is fairly straightforward, but a couple of sections should be noted. First, notice the difference between the damage calculation for a herbivore and a carnivore. Herbivores can only use defense if they are defending, whereas carnivores can use defense if they are not attacking and can attack if attacking. Second, we add a fairly significant reward when a creature kills another creature. While this may appear rather bloodthirsty, we need to do so in order to train killers. Feel free to play with this reward if you want a more peaceful terrarium.

 The rule calculations here are arbitrary since the original source for Microsoft Terrarium could not be found. If you are in possession of the original code, please contact the author.

5. Finally, add the new `Defend` method, as follows:

```
void Defend()
{
  currentAction = "Defend";
  nextAction = Time.timeSinceLevelLoad + (25 / MaxSpeed);
}
```

6. The `Defend` method is quite simple and all it does it set the creature to `Defend`.

7. Be sure to save the file when you are done editing it and return to Unity. Make sure that there are no compiler errors.

Now that we have the required code changes in our `CreatureAgent` file to support the `CreatureType` carnivore, in the next section we will build the carnivore agent in the terrarium.

Building the carnivore

Building the carnivore creature will follow many of the same patterns we used for the plant and herbivore creatures. Open up Unity and follow this exercise to put the carnivore into the scene:

1. Select the **HerbivoreBrain** in the **Hierarchy** window and type *Ctrl + D* (*Command + D* on macOS) to duplicate the object. Rename the new object `CarnivoreBrain`.

2. Duplicate the **Herbivore** creature agent object and rename the new object **Carnivore**.

3. Open the **Carnivore** object and select the **Chicken** model. Type `Delete` to delete the model.

4. Drag the **Dragon** prefab from the `Assets/_Gloomy_Animal/Meshes` folder and drop it onto the **Carnivore** object in the **Hierarchy** window.

5. Set the properties on all the **Carnivore** components as shown in the following screenshot:

Setting the properties of the Dragon (Carnivore)

6. Be sure to create the **Carnivore** prefab in the `Assets/Terrarium/Prefabs` folder and set the **Child Spawn** property.

7. In order to balance things out, our carnivore is going to need to eat more than one herbivore. Therefore, duplicate more herbivores and plants into the scene. Five herbivores, five plants, and one carnivore is a good starting balance.

8. Launch the Build Settings dialog and build the scene for external training.

The whole process of putting the carnivore into the terrarium should go quite quickly now given that you have had some practice. That leaves our next section to train the carnivore and run our terrarium in full mode.

Training the carnivore

As you may have already guessed, the carnivore training is going to be fairly close as to what we did with the plant eaters. Follow along with this exercise to train the carnivore:

1. Open Visual Studio Code or another text editor and load the `trainer_config.yaml` file.

2. Add the **CarnivoreBrain** settings, essentially a clone of the **HerbivoreBrain** settings, to the end of the file, as shown in the following code:

```
CarnivoreBrain:
    use_recurrent: true
    sequence_length: 64
    num_layers: 1
    hidden_units: 128
    memory_size: 512
    beta: 1.0e-2
    gamma: 0.99
    num_epoch: 3
    buffer_size: 1024
    batch_size: 128
    max_steps: 5.0e5
    summary_freq: 500
    time_horizon: 128
```

3. Save the file when you are done editing it.

4. Open a Python or Anaconda prompt and activate `ml-agents`. Change to the `ml-agents` folder.

5. Run the trainer with the following command:

```
python python/learn.py python/python.exe --run-id=terrarium2 --train
--slow
```

6. You will notice that things may not balance out very quickly. This because the carnivore needs a bit more training and intelligence, if you will. It is the same in nature, where we often see that the predator has a higher capacity for thinking.

7. Switch the camera around and watch how the Dragon (carnivore) picks up hunting. It may take them a while and they may die a few times. The following screenshot shows a sample terrarium running:

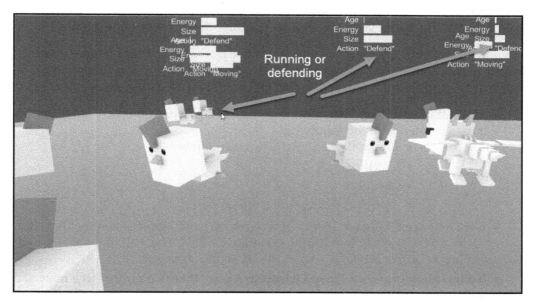

Herbivore creatures learning new actions to avoid the carnivore

You will also notice that the herbivore begins to pick new strategies in order to avoid getting eaten. In the preceding excerpt, you can see how they run from the scary dragon.

That concludes all the time we have for this example, but it really is far from finished. Feel free to add to this project and share it with your friends. You could even create competitions to train and compete with the agents in the terrarium just like the old Microsoft Terrarium contest. In the last section, we will discuss how you can proceed with your learning and other areas to develop in with your new-found knowledge.

Next steps

Your immediate next steps will of course be to make sure that you complete a couple of the suggested exercises at the end of this and the earlier chapters. There really is no better way to reinforce learning than by doing; take a cue from our learning agents. If you have time, look to build on or use another new example using ML-Agents.

Outside of your learning and this book, you have just begun a journey in a new wave of programming. It would not be surprising that in the near future (25 years or so) that programming becomes a lost art. After all, would you rather write a bunch of code or write an agent that writes your code better, faster, and even automatically has it tested? Yeah, no contest really. Therefore, if you are under 30 and reading this book, don't plan on programming for the rest of your life, look to teaching the programming agents.

With that in mind, what are the skills you should be pursuing in order to give you true mastery of reinforcement learning and your ML career in general? The following is a list of what appear to be the most requested skills that could get you a job teaching ML-Agents:

- **Math**: It may be hard, but it is the path to ML glory. At the very least, you should have knowledge in the following:
    - Probability and Statistics (fundamental)
    - Calculus
    - 3D
    - Tensor Calculus and prerequistes
- **Data Science**: There are plenty of free courses and materials online that train the basics all the way up to building complex models. You will likely waste less time buying a course or books, so consider that option as well.
- **Neural Networks and Deep Learning**: Again, there's plenty of free material online that can teach you the basics but again, you get what you pay for and what you are willing to put into learning.
- **Reinforcement Learning**: RL is quickly evolving and it is quite likely that some of the techniques in this book could become stale quickly. Therefore, trust that working in RL is going to require constant learning of new techniques and innovations.

Building on your skills will take a lifetime, so always plan on learning. In the meantime, if you are looking for some new projects to throw ML-Agents at, here are some thoughts:

- **Self-driving and robotics**: Why are we still letting robot makers drive their own bots? Seriously, isn't a bigger challenge also adding intelligence? Perhaps RobotWars AI? In any case, Unity provides the ability to simulate training of robotic agents in a multitude of scenarios.
- **Gaming**: Well of course, but what about games where people train agents? Perhaps not unlike the little Tamagochi devices that were carried around in the 90s.
- **AR/VR/MR**: Integrating these technologies with reality experiences can provide ways for an augmented agent to perhaps assist a person in day to day activities.
- **Industrial simulations/augmentations**: Businesses are discovering not only the power of 3D but the ability for Unity to support many wide and varied platforms seamlessly. This has caused a whole new growing trend of in-house business/industrial apps are being used from warehouses to hospitals. All are potential candidates for some form of smart agent scenario.

The preceding examples are really only the start of what is possible and the limits at this point are really only your imagination. We leave the rest up to you and we hope that you enjoy your learning journey.

 The author of this book is always excited to hear about projects that were developed by readers. Please be sure to look up **Micheal Lanham** (note the spelling of the first name) on LinkedIn and share your content.

Exercises

Try to complete at least one of the following exercises on your own. Using the skills you just learned only reinforces your learning, and you should really appreciate that concept by now. Do an exercise; your brain will thank you later:

1. Create a variety of different **plant** species, each with different points. If you are very ambitious, build different prefabs and use other models to represent different species.
2. Create a variety of different **herbivore** species, each with different points and perhaps different models. Do your new animals perform better or worse?

3. Create a variety of different **carnivore** species again with different points and other models. Feel free to download other free poly models on your own and use those.

4. Encourage your friends or colleagues to build agents and see who can build and train the best creature. You can share this by exporting your creature prefab from Unity and then importing it into another game.

5. Convert the agents to use Visual Observations from the Vector Observation they are using. How much more difficult will this make the training?

6. The original Terrarium also allowed for agent communication. We omitted that due to time, but add the ability for similar species to communicate in some manner.

7. Build a fully connected peer to peer terrarium that allows creatures to hop among peers. If you can build this, your skills are way beyond this book and you likely work at Unity now.

Summary

In our final chapter together, we built a larger multi-agent training scenario called Terrarium, modeled after the original Microsoft Terrarium, a developer game developed by Microsoft in 2002 as a way of promoting the security features of .NET. We first spent time understanding the old rules and theme of the original game and those rules our creature agents would need to follow when building our simulation. From there, we pulled down some useful assets to make our simulation a little more game-like. Then, we built the foundations of our terrarium and created our first creature, the plant. The plant is essential to the life and training of our higher level agents like the herbivore, which was the next creature we built and started training as an ML-Agent in our scene. After building the herbivore, we moved onto building a carnivore creature as a way to balance and finish up our terrarium. Finally, we looked at suggestions for your next steps in training and other possible ideas for some exciting projects that use ML-Agents.

It is our hope that this book gives you the confidence to build on your knowledge and create stunning simulations, games, and apps that use ML-Agents to their full potential. This version of the book is only for the beta version, but the foundations of knowledge you have built will carry with you to your other pursuits in AI.

Other Books You May Enjoy

If you enjoyed this book, you may be interested in these other books by Packt:

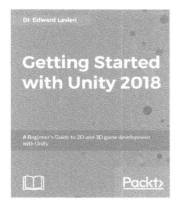

Getting Started with Unity 2018 - Third Edition
Dr. Edward Lavieri

ISBN: 978-1-78883-010-2

- Set up your Unity development environment and navigate its tools
- Import and use custom assets and asset packages to add characters to your game
- Build a 3D game world with a custom terrain, water, sky, mountains, and trees
- Animate game characters, using animation controllers, and scripting
- Apply audio and particle effects to the game
- Create intuitive game menus and interface elements
- Customize your game with sound effects, shadows, lighting effects, and rendering options
- Debug code and provide smooth error handling

Unity Virtual Reality Projects - Second Edition
Jonathan Linowes

ISBN: 978-1-78847-880-9

- Create 3D scenes with Unity and other 3D tools while learning about world space and scale
- Build and run VR applications for specific headsets, including Oculus, Vive, and Daydream
- Interact with virtual objects using eye gaze, hand controllers, and user input events
- Move around your VR scenes using locomotion and teleportation
- Implement an audio fireball game using physics and particle systems
- Implement an art gallery tour with teleportation and data info
- Design and build a VR storytelling animation with a soundtrack and timelines
- Create social VR experiences with Unity networking

Leave a review - let other readers know what you think

Please share your thoughts on this book with others by leaving a review on the site that you bought it from. If you purchased the book from Amazon, please leave us an honest review on this book's Amazon page. This is vital so that other potential readers can see and use your unbiased opinion to make purchasing decisions, we can understand what our customers think about our products, and our authors can see your feedback on the title that they have worked with Packt to create. It will only take a few minutes of your time, but is valuable to other potential customers, our authors, and Packt. Thank you!

Index

www.ingramcontent.com/pod-product-compliance
Lightning Source LLC
Chambersburg PA
CBHW080527060326
40690CB00022B/5057